Copyright

Contents

Introduction

This book on domain investment has been a work in progress for the last few years. I've been building my own library of everything that I've learned about domain names. These little insights have been written on various notebooks post-it notes and word documents.

I started to write down these pieces of information after Warner Bros bought the first ever domain name that I owned. It was not a very big sale, but it made me realize that people actually pay money for domain names.

It was not long after my euphoria of actually selling something that I made my first mistake. I registered and bought hundreds of worthless domain names, trademarked terms and typo domains. I was convinced that, just like before, people would come to me and offer money to buy one of my domains.

Of course, I was wrong. I learned the hard way that not all domains are created as equal. I slowly started to read domain name blogs, and spent hundreds of hours researching domain names and who buys them.

I still made no money! After years of this, I thought that I'd finished in domaining. Then I had an epiphany: buy domain names that companies *need* in order to succeed online!

Keyword domain names, domain upgrades, any domain name that I'd be able to sell to a company that I know could help improve their online presence. Obvious, right?

I started my new business model, and the sales started coming in. The model was successful and repeatable, and so I carried on with it. Then, at the beginning of the year – after closing my biggest domain name sale ever ($10,000 sale from a domain name that I bought for $69*) I decided to gather all of these scraps of paper and put them into a book.

This is book is here to try and help you avoid many of the mistakes that I have made. These mistakes have cost me hundreds, if not thousands of dollars. I lost money through domain names for a very long time because of my mistakes.

I hope that by making this eBook, it puts you on the track to make some extra income, which will hopefully lead to you making a living from domain names one day. The book will not only show you how to make money with buying and selling domains, but it'll also help you with developing your domain names into profitable websites.

My book is not a get rich quick solution. It will not tell you how to make $1million this year. So if that is what you were expecting, then sorry, but you'll be disappointed. What it will show you, however, is everything that I've learned about domain names. From the very basics of domain names to which domains you should buy, and how to sell them for maximum profit.

I want to help you create some extra income for yourself from one of the most fascinating, unpredictable and potentially profitable industries ever.

Let's get started.

*This sale is 100% real. I have all the relevant documents to prove I sold the domain name for $10,000 – which I bought months earlier for $69. I have bought hundreds of domain names over the years. This is the first time I've ever managed to do something like this. So, please don't expect any "domain flips" of this magnitude!

What You Need:

As a new domain investor, here's what you need:

- Daily access to a computer
- Patience
- Money – even if it's $100, that's enough to start domaining. You can't realistically start by registering a domain for $8.
- More patience
- A couple of hours every day to work on domain names

What you Don't Need:

- An ego – it will soon be deflated. You'll quickly realize you know nothing. I did.
- Prior experience of computers or domain names
- Coding experience – for our websites (covered later in the book), we'll be using WordPress, so no coding or development experience is necessary.
- Staff – this is something you need to do yourself for now. You can't just outsource it, and hope that someone else can make you money!

Chapter 1: Domain Name Basics

As this book is designed for everyone from an Internet whiz-kid to his Grandma to read, I wanted to give a basic overview of what domain names are and what they do.

If this is too simplified for you, please skip to part two where I will introduce you to domain name ages, finding keywords, niches and more.

What Is a Domain Name?

A domain name – quite simply – is a human-friendly address. The Internet is built on Internet Protocols (IP) addresses, which are strings of numbers that host a website.

Example: 74.125.157.99 is the IP address for Google.

The human brain finds it easier to memorize words than a string of random numbers. So, domain names were used to solve the problem. Instead of typing in 74.125.157.99, you would simply type www.google.com.

A domain is made up of anywhere from 1 to 64 characters, numbers and hyphens followed by the domain extension (TLD).

.aero .asia .biz .cat .com .coop .edu .gov .info .int .jobs .mil .mobi .museum .name .net .org .pro .tel .travel .xxx

List of TLDs, according to the IANA (Internet Assigned Numbers Authority)

TLDs

Top Level Domains (TLDs) are the domain extensions: .com, .net, .org, .info to name but a few. All TLDs are not created equally. The most popular extension by a long way is .com – with around 114,000,000 .com domain names registered to date.

The first domain name to be registered was a .COM domain name – Symbolics.com in 1985. Since then, those 114,000,000 .com domains have been registered. Along the way, the .COM domain name has produced some pretty amazing sales:

- Sex.com - $13,000,000
- Fund.com - $9,999,950
- Porn.com - $9,500,000
- FB.com - $8,500,000
- Diamond.com - $7,500,000

In fact, the 54 largest reported domain sales ever (according to www.domaining.com/topsales) were .COM domains.

It's partly for this reason that the .com extension is the TLD that I'd recommend you stick with for now. 95% of my portfolio are .com domains because of one simple fact: I've found that I can sell them far more easily – consumers are more aware of .COM domains than any other extension, and so companies will pay vast sums of money to get a god .COM domain name.

In the past, the other "major TLD" has been .Net. Prices have typically always been lower for .Net names, but they did sell well, especially to companies who couldn't afford a top .COM domain. As of 2015, I believe that .NET domain name prices are declining thanks to the emergence of the new batch of TLDs (explained below). These new TLDs mean that there are far more and far cheaper alternatives to .Net, hence the loss of value. When I first started buying domain names, I bought a lot of 3-Letter .NET domain names, which all sold well. Now however, those domains have largely lost most of their value. Of course, there are still .NET domains and other TLDs which buck the trend, producing the occasional big sale, but from a new investors point of view, .COM is a safe bet for now.

If you turn on your TV and look at the next commercial break, you'll see that most companies use a .com domain to advertise their product. Especially in the USA. There is still an active market for .COM domain names, and I read many articles every week showing the .COM acquisitions of medium-large companies around the world. In some other countries, however, ccTLDs are sometimes preferred over .COM domains. In the UK for example, .CO.UK is used widely by smallmedium businesses. .CO.UK is an example of a ccTLD.

ccTLDs

Country-Code Top Level Domains (ccTLDs) are domain extensions used by individual countries. Whilst you may not have been aware of ccTLDs, you'll have come across them in some way.

- Social bookmarking website Delicious.com started out by using the ccTLD .us (del.icio.us) · Last FM uses the .fm ccTLD.
- The URL shortening service Bitly uses the .ly ccTLD

.co.uk - United Kingdom, .ly - Libya, .me - Montenegro, .la - Laos, .ky - Cayman Islands, .jp - Japan, .ie - Northern Ireland, .fr - France, .es - Spain

A list of 9 ccTLD domain extensions. There are hundreds.

Website owners in countries other than the USA sometimes prefer to use ccTLDs over .COM domain names. Many Search Engine Optimization (SEO) experts have said that companies targeting certain countries will get a higher ranking by using that countries' ccTLD. For example, Amazon UK would use amazon.co.uk rather than amazon.com.

Consumers in certain countries often perceive ccTLDs as being more trustworthy than a .COM website. In China for example, citizens have a tendency to visit a .CN website over .COM websites. This could be due to language preferences or the locality of the website's staff.

From an investors point of view, there are many people who do make a living from buying and selling ccTLDs. Usually that involves buying and selling the ccTLD of their country. For example, a Canadian domain investor may own a certain percentage of .CA domain names. Some investors do well from owning ccTLD domain names and can build a steady income.

For someone who is new to domain investing, I'd would not recommend buying ccTLD domain names, as there is a higher risk in owning this type of domain than investing in a .COM domain name. Aside from this, you're essentially restricted on who you can sell to. A .COM can be sold to anyone, anywhere. However, if we take the .CA domain as an example, there won't be too many people outside of Canada who would want to buy a .CA domain, so your potential market is far smaller.

Why TLDs Matter

The TLD that you choose to invest in has a big impact on the resale value of your domain name. As a rule, .COM domains are valued highest, followed by other TLDs such as .NET, .XYZ, .ORG and some ccTLDs such as .ME and .CO.

A perfect example of why TLDs matter is Porn.com. The domain Porn.com sold in May 2007 for
$9.5million. In January 2008, Porn.net sold for $400,000 – around a 94% difference in value between Porn.com and Porn.net.

This is similar real estate. A house in The Hampton's
(our .com) is much more desirable than a house in Brownsville (our .net). Therefore, the house in the Hampton's is much more expensive.

This won't be the last real estate analogy that you see. There are many similarities between the domain name industry and the real estate industry. Both have rules and regulations, and both have their own "recipe for success".

New gTLDs

In October 2013, the first of over 300 "New gTLDs" was created. There are plenty of individuals and businesses who complain that there are no good .COM domain names left. They're right. It's because of this reason that aftermarket prices for .COM domains are increasing out of the reach of most of these frustrated buyers with small budgets.

.Dentist, .London, .NYC, .XYZ, .Club, .Ninja, .World, .Wiki

A few of the new gTLD domain names, released by ICANN

The New gTLD releases were billed as the savior of the Internet – the new .COM boom. Everyone will be able to afford these new gTLD prices, and small and large businesses alike will flock towards these new gTLDs and leave .COM behind.

I'm writing this in early 2015, and so far this hasn't happened. There are around 1400 new gTLDs which have been released, or are scheduled to be released. From reading many articles and statistics about new gTLDs, it seems that in general companies haven't taken to them as expected.

I do believe that there will be some growth in extensions such as .XYZ, .LONDON, .CLUB, .NYC and .WEB but many of the others are struggling to attract new registrations.

I have avoided investing in these domain names, and have continued to invest in .COM domain names instead. I believe that consumers have been exposed to .COM domains for so long that many will not be aware that other gTLDs even exists. It'll take many years of exposure and marketing for new gTLDs to get to the stage that .COM is at.

What Is Domaining?

Domaining (domain investing) is the practice of buying and selling Internet Domain names. There are two main monetization methods for domain names: buy a domain and sell it for a higher price, and buy a domain and generate income from it.

The first method involves buying a domain name (probably an expired domain), and reselling it for a higher price.

The second method involves buying a domain name and placing either adverts or a full website on it. You'll use this website to produce a monthly revenue, which hopefully will cover the cost of your original outlay plus the domain name's renewal fees.

In this sense, domain investing is very much like investing in real estate. You can buy a property and make a monthly income from renting out a property whilst still retaining your ownership of the property, or you can buy a property and sell (flip) it for a higher price.

An example of domain flipping would be a domain name that I bought in August 2014 and sold in October 2014 for 14 times what I paid for it. I did nothing to the domain name at all apart from finding someone who was willing to buy the domain name from me.

An example of domain development would be a domain name that I bought for $260 in January 2013. I built a website, and by the beginning of March 2013 I had a lead generation partnership in place with a company that would pay me $50 per lead. I made back my initial investment inside a month.

The Domain Name Lifecycle

If you are going to be buying and selling domain names, you need to know about the typical domain name lifecycle – from registration to deletion. The first thing you should know is that a domain name is not technically owned by you. Even Facebook.com, or Google.com are not owned by Facebook or Google respectively.

Every domain is rented at an annual cost. If you register a domain name, you have the right to use that domain name for the length of time you've registered the domain name for (one year, five years, ten years). You can choose to renew the domain name for as many years as you like. If you choose not to renew your domain, that domain name is rereleased, where it is available for someone else to register.

Here's a useful chart that I've put together to show the domain name lifecycle in simple terms:

Active Domain Name:
This is the first stage of a domain name's life. The domain name is available to register from any domain name registrar. You can register these domain names for between 1 and 10 years.

Expired Domain Name:
Once the registration period has lapsed, the domain expires. The registrar will usually hold onto the domain for you, to prevent your website from going down. You can still renew the domain name at this point.

Domain Name Redemption Period:
This is a 30 day period which occurs after the domain name has expired. During this time, the domain registrar keeps ahold of the domain name rather than allowing it to immediately delete.

Pending Delete:
If a domain name has gone through the redemption period, it hasn't been renewed by the original registrant, and it hasn't been "caught" by anyone else, then it enters a Pending Delete phase for 5 days.

Available For Registration

Can you still register a good domain name?

Define a good domain? I was able to register a domain name for a client last year. It cost them $7, and was the only domain name they wanted for the launch of a new venture. That to them was a good domain, and it was available to register. As a domainer, that wouldn't have been a name that I'd have registered in the hope of flipping.

From an investors point of view, I personally say stick to "aftermarket" or "expired" domains (explanations later on). This is because there are already 114 million .com domain names registered, and to get any domain name that is going to be resalable has more than likely already been registered. To buy these types of names, you are going to have to look at expired domain names.

New domain investors often get lured in on the attraction of registering domain names for $8 and selling them on for a large profit. Let me dispel this strategy here and now. Blindly registering domain names for $8 apiece in the hope that someone will buy one of your names is not the right way to start domain investing. It's an excellent way to lose money straight away. Most domain investors, for that reason, invest in expired domain names.

One of the main topics in this book will be expired domain names. We'll cover this topic in great depth later on in the book. However, I wanted to give you a brief explanation of an expired domain name, and why they can be so valuable.

Expired domains are domains names that have lapsed in registration. Most domain names which expire are worthless, and eventually end up being returned to the registry. However, some still hold a value, and can be sold on to another company if you know how.

If you've read the section about the Domain Name Lifecycle, you'll notice that I said that anyone can catch a domain name during the redemption period. This is done by backordering a domain name with a Drop Catching service. There are many available. The most popular are NameJet, SnapNames and Pool.com.

Once the domain name has expired, these services will try to acquire the domain name for you. Backordering costs are usually $69. However, if a domain name is backordered by more than one person – which happens a lot – then it may be put up for auction, where ultimately the highest bidder will own the domain name.

The Future of .COM

With the emergence of apps, new gTLDs and the increasing influence of Google on the way people access information, you may be asking whether .COM domain names, and in fact domains in general are going to be worth anything in the future.

It's a good question, and I can only answer from my point of view based on evidence and sales. If you take a look at DNJournal.com, you'll see that every single week there are high priced domain name sales reported (there are many more unreported). Every year there are multiple million dollar sales– there were 11 reported sales of over $1m in 2014. As for domain sales over $100,000, there were 73 reported sales in 2014.

That number seems to be rising year on year. According to IDNX.com, the leading domain pricing index, domain names have gained 25% in value over the last year.

With the emergence of new gTLDs, I see premium .COM domain names becoming even more valuable. Less valuable .COM domain names may continue to decline in value as small businesses have more options when it comes to TLDs. As for apps–there will always be a need for domain names for websites and promotions to go alongside those apps.

Domain Appraisals

I wanted to write about domain appraisals in the first chapter, as I believe it's something that many rookies get drawn into. Domain appraisals are basically the price that either a person or a piece of software thinks that your domain name is worth. As far as software domain appraisals go, there is generally a wide gap between the appraised value and an actual sales price. Some are accurate, but some are highly inaccurate.

A typical domain appraisal website uses parameters such as

- CPC (cost per click)
- Keyword data
- Past sales
- Type in traffic

These parameters will reveal a dollar value for each domain name.

To test out automated domain appraisals, I put 10 random recently sold domain names into Valuate.com's appraisal website. Here are the results:

24

Domain Name	Actual Sale Price	Valuate.com Appraisal
345.com	$800,000	$31,000
ExerciseBike.com	$20,000	$241,000
NewMedia.com	$18,000	$90,000
Encinitas.com	$48,000	$57,000
FindYourCalling.com	$30,000	$680
HelloSocial.com	$25,000	$2,300
Problem.com	$35,200	$208,000
Reported.com	$19,999	$30,000
TV.ae	$95,000	$0
Rides.com	$120,000	$123,000

As you can see, the automated appraisals were pretty accurate on 2 domain names – Rides.com and Encinitas.com. As for the rest, the appraisals didn't even come close the actual domain sale price.

Take these automated appraisals with a pinch of salt.

Automated domain names can be valuable to see whether the domains you hold have any value at all. If you have a larger portfolio, this can be a useful way to see which domains to keep and which to drop. They'll never be completely accurate, but are worth looking at. The two largest domain appraisal websites are Estibot.com and Valuate.com.

There are plenty of companies who offer human domain appraisal services. Meaning that for a certain price, a staff member will evaluate your domain name and tell you how much they think it's worth. I never use domain appraisals from any company as I believe this they will never accurately value your domain name.

All they can do is charge you a fee for giving their opinion based on certain parameters – largely the same as an automated appraisal which was mentioned above.

Domain Appraisal Scams

Domain appraisal scams are an old trick used to try to get money from you by requesting a domain appraisal on a domain name you own. Here's how a typical domain appraisal scam works:

1. The scammer sends you an email telling you they'd like to buy your domain name

2. You send back a price, and they agree. You get excited at the thought of what you'll do with all of that money you're about to receive.

3. Before they send over the money for the domain, they want to get an appraisal of your domain name from a trusted source.

4. They give you a link to either the appraisal website itself or a "blog" showing you the value of domain appraisals. Either way, the scammer will own both of these websites.

5. You go to the domain appraisal website and pay someone to appraise your domain name.

6. You send the appraisal to the scammer, but you never hear from them again. They have your money, and you have a worthless appraisal.

I've been caught out by this type of domain appraisal scam in the past. In my defense, I'd only just started to buy and sell domains. I'd just bought a domain name that I thought would sell well, and a few weeks later I was pleased to see what I thought was an offer for the domain name in my inbox.

The "buyer" was interested in acquiring the domain, and I immediately responded with a price of $35,000.
They agreed to buy the domain name on one condition:

I get it appraised. Being a naïve know-it-all, I bought the appraisal, which cost over $100, and subsequently never heard from the buyer again.

It was an expensive lesson to learn when you have very limited funds to start with. You do still see these emails being sent out, so please be careful. You should never need to pay for a domain appraisal.

Since then I've dealt with hundreds of genuine buyers from startups to Fortune 500 companies. The words "domain appraisal" have never been mentioned in any conversations.

Domain Name Glossary

I wanted to include a glossary of terms used in domaining, because in the rest of this book you may find words and phrases which you are unsure of. I couldn't do a better job than DomainSherpa.com's "Domain Name Dictionary", so here is a link:

http://www.domainsherpa.com/domain-namedictionary/

Bookmark the site and visit it whenever you're unsure of a domain related word. Whilst you're there, why not watch an interview or two? When you're ready, we'll move on to the next chapter.

Chapter 2: The Anatomy of a Good Domain Name

Just before we delve into the world of domaining, I wanted to just explain to you what I believe is classed as a good domain name. This is my own opinion, based on what someone who's new to domain investing may want to invest in. A good domain name isn't just a name that sounds good to you. It needs to be backed up by a series of facts and statistics to give yourself the best possible chance of making money from it.

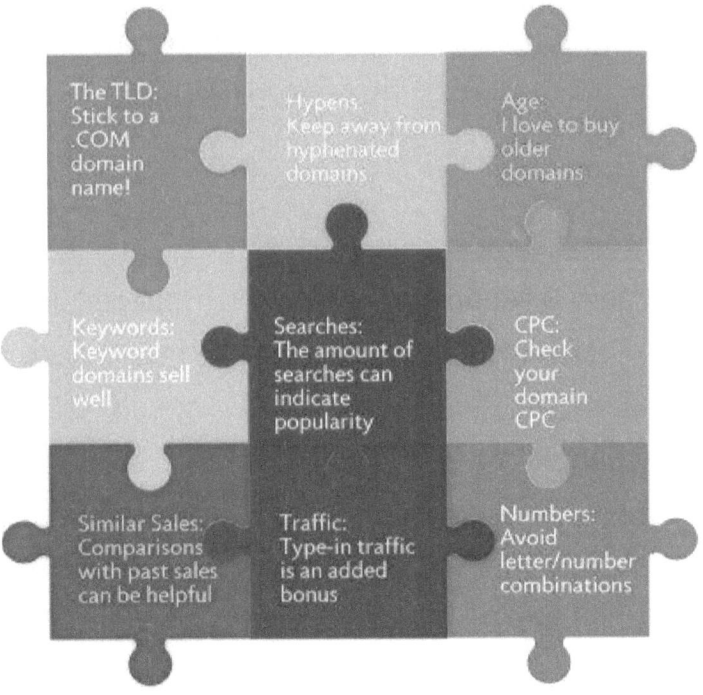

Of course, you may well have a different view on what constitutes a good domain name. That's fine – we're all different (fortunately!).

1. **The TLD:** The domain name extension is important in finding a good domain name. I believe that the best domain names are .COM domains. There are always exceptions: there are good .net domains, there are good .org domains, there are good new TLD domains (for example, coffee.club was sold recently for $100k over a 10 year period), and there are good ccTLD domain names. However, as a rule I'd always say .COM is king! Out of the 100 largest reported domain name sales of 2014, 79 were .COM domain names. 3 were .NET and1 was .ORG. That should tell you what is selling well.

2. **Hyphens & Numbers:** Always avoid hyphened domains as investments unless you are in Germany. According to a recent study, half of all German TLD (.DE) registrations have a hyphen in, and many German Internet users expect domain names to include hyphens. As for numbers, they can be valuable when grouped together – for example 2000.com. The price

of 3 and 4 character numerical domain names has risen drastically over the past couple of years, thanks largely to domain investors from China.

It's important to understand the approaches that different countries and cultures have to the Internet. The two examples I've given you above – Germany and China – are both prime examples of the fact that awareness of other cultures can be beneficial to your domain investments.

3. **Age:** This factor isn't as important as it once was. Age used to be important when trying to rank a website on Google, but recent changes have meant that content is far more important than age. From an investment point of view, I don't like to own domain names that are less than 4/5 years old. There are plenty of benefits to aged domain names: existing type in traffic, more valuable keywords/combinations and small SEO advantages. In fact, looking through my portfolio I've noticed a large majority are domain names registered between the late 1990s and early 2000s.

4. **Keywords:** Keywords can be extremely important in a good domain name, especially when developing the

domain or selling it on. Descriptive keyword domain names can come under this category, too. Descriptive domains are exact

match keywords for industries and professions, such as LandscapeArchitect.com.

5. **Searches:** Before buying a domain name, go to Google's Keyword Planner and see how many searches the domain's keywords/phrase gets per month. It's always worth checking on how many searches a set of keywords gets. It's often a good sign of a popular term, niche or market. If a keyword/phrase gets hundreds or thousands of searches per month on Google, it's probably a good domain name.

That doesn't necessarily mean that domains with low searches are worthless. Search numbers are just another factor to take into consideration.

6. **Niche:** Exploring the niche can be a good way of determining the value of a domain name. If it is a product domain, for example, does that product have good online sales? Do companies advertise for the

keywords? Who are the biggest companies in the niche? What is their advertising budget per month? All of this information is available online, and we'll cover most of it later in the book.

7. **Similar Sales:** Comparing your domain name is interesting to do. It shouldn't necessarily determine your pricing for the domain name you own, but it can give an indication to what companies or investors are willing to pay. Use websites such as NameBio.com or DNSalePrice.com to discover historical sales data.

8. **Traffic:** Does your domain name receive visitors every day? Type in traffic can tell you a lot about a domain name, and can also add value. The most popular generic domain names on the Internet receive thousands of type-in visitors per day. It's no coincidence that they sell for millions of dollars apiece, however – don't get caught up on traffic statistics. The vast majority of domain names are sold without knowledge of their traffic statistics.

There was an article in the New York Times which I remember reading which stated that direct navigation traffic (or type in traffic) is the most valuable type of traffic for a company. The owner of diapers.com, for example, will receive a number of direct navigation visits from parents looking for diapers, and as such, a lot of these visits will convert into sales.

9. **Price:** One of the most important factors to take into consideration when buying a domain name is the price. Overspending on a domain name can mean that you have no opportunity to make money on the domain name.

Buying a domain name through an auction can be a prime example on overspending on a domain name. After researching your domain name, and knowing what your budget is, you don't want to be drawn into a bidding war which goes well above your original budget.

Chapter 3: Valuable Information You Need To Know

If you are looking to make millions of dollars and retire to a life of freedom, fun and travel, then stop reading. Domaining isn't for you – maybe try the lottery.

Domaining (the art of buying and selling domain names) is a tough industry, but ultimately it can be very rewarding. Once you get your first domain sale, you'll realize that the work is worth it.

What domaining isn't:

- It isn't a 9 to 5 job
- It isn't a get rich quick scheme
- It isn't for everyone
- It isn't cyber squatting

What domaining is:

- It is rewarding
- It is a 24/7/365 industry

- It is a good long term investment (with the right names)
- It is interesting
- It is a community of ~~geeks~~ people just like you
- It opens up new opportunities and partnerships.

How Not To Start

You'll hear many success stories in the domain industry, but only a few are willing to show where they started. I started domain investing a couple of years ago, and I started in the worst way possible. I bought one trademarked domain name and a lot of 64 domain names on eBay. I can still remember some of the domains that I bought. The domain names I owned at the time included:

- Riuven.co.uk – I still have no idea why I bought this
- Chipmunks2.com – I read that Fox were making a 2nd Alvin and the Chipmunks film. I thought I could cash in on this.
- IphoneWhite.co.uk – A trademark, which I should have avoided.
- BannerCommerce.net –

> Probably the best of a very bad
> bunch.

- Reviews2u.com – Another terrible domain
- Cheatcodezpro.com – Just no.

I had no prior knowledge of what made a good domain name. I had no prior knowledge of the Internet, really. As such, I made a lot of mistakes which cost a lot of money. I can't remember the actual figure, and I don't want to work it out as it'll be too depressing, but I think it was in the thousands.

Needless to say, I never received a single offer on any domain name I owned at the time. I ended up dropping all of the domains that I'd bought, and learned a very valuable lesson. Don't rush in and buy domain names when you don't know what you're doing.

I assumed that I would be able to sell any domain name for a profit. I did try to sell all of these names for ridiculous prices (would you pay $5,000 for any of these names?), but as you might have guessed, I sold none of them.

This is the perfect example of how not to start. There is a famous quote which says: "Only a fool learns from his own mistakes. The wise man learns from the mistakes of others." Be the wise man, learn from my mistakes.

This book should be a good starting place for you, but it shouldn't be the end of your domain education. Reading blogs, articles and domain related websites every day is the only way to stay up to date with an industry which is moving quickly.

Aside from reading this book, you will also find great pieces of advice from websites such as DomainSherpa.com, DomainInvesting.com, TheDomains.com, DomainNameWire.com and DNJournal.com. Each of these websites offer something different, but each are extremely valuable resources. Learning to read daily about domain names is a step in the right direction and an excellent use of your time. Read, learn, repeat.

What type of domain name you could buy

If you navigate to DNJournal.com, and take a look at their weekly sales chart, you'll notice a large majority of the domain names which are sold every week are .COM domains. This should tell you that your best bet is to invest in .COM domains.

However, as I have shown you above, it's not enough to simply register or buy some .COM domain names and hope that someone will buy them. Knowing what to invest in is the key. I'm going to list some of my recommendations for investments. These are only recommendations, and I can't be held responsible for what you buy, and for how much you pay.

3 Letter .COM Domains

These are expensive domain names to buy, but are very liquid domains. Meaning that if you do need to cash in a domain name quickly, you'll be able to fairly easily. There seems to be a large pool of domain investors looking to buy 3-Letter .com domains. These domains are also becoming increasingly popular with companies looking to stand out from the crowd, and regularly appear on DNJournal's list of Top Domain Sales.

Typically, a 3 letter .COM will sell for around $7,000$15,000 so it's not something to invest in immediately, but something to keep in mind for the future.

Of course, there are certain criteria which make certain 3-Letter .com domains more valuable than others. These criteria can be found at "http://www.3character.com/priceguide.html"

Two Word .COM Domains

Two word .com domain names can sell very well. I love a good two-word domain, for example: StayCool.com was a domain name that I bought from a user on DNForum. I later sold it to Jockey International Inc. Not all two word .com domains are created equally, however.

Descriptive keywords and phrases are often useful assets for companies, but you need to know how to pick the domain names, and how much to pay for them. There are excellent opportunities in this type of domain names, but you really have to pick your names well. Professional domains work well too (I picked up LandscapeArchitect.com recently).

Two Word .COM domain names can be picked up for a relatively small amount. I've sold many in the last few years – WellbeingCoach.com, TanningFranchise.com, BrownLumber.com to name but a few. Each was picked up for less than $100. It's important to do research before buying any two word .com. Look at whether there are many companies using those keywords or that phrase, and whether there are any advertisers for the keywords/phrase.

Another category which I think works well are what I like to call imperative domain names. Authoritative domain names using imperative grammar. The example above – StayCool.com is an imperative domain. Other examples would be CallNow.com and BuyThis.com.

Chinese Domain Names

This isn't a market I've got into yet, but I'm looking to invest this year. China has produced more billionaires and millionaires than any country except for the USA, and many are turning their attention to domain name investments.

To a lot of people, investing in domain names for the Chinese market is a difficult thing. However, there are plenty of guides online about investing in Chinese domain names. The website I'm using at the moment is ChineseLandrush.com. They have some interesting points.

Geographical Domains

This type of name is a firm favorite of mine. Some city + profession domain names are good investments. Real estate domain names (such as TorontoRealEstate.com) are often sought after, and can provide a good return on investment. A few things to check before buying one, though:

1. What is the population of the city? Domains for cities with a high population are always good.
2. Which profession is it? Is it a profession which spends a lot of money online? Real estate and dentistry are both professions

    that typically spend a lot of money on websites, SEO and online advertising.

You want to be aware of which niche you're buying into. I've found that niches such as Real Estate and Dentistry can sell well. I haven't had as much success with Doctor domain names, Electrician domain names or Florist domain names.

Another excellent aspect of a geographical domain is that you can easily create what's called a lead generation site. A local lead generation site allows you to create a website and send the sales leads to a local company, who'll then pay you an agreed amount of money to acquire the lead for their own purposes. I have done this with a couple of websites and have had good success. I'll be producing a small guide towards the end of this book to show you how this is done.

Brandable Domains/Startup Domains

Brandable domain names are extremely popular at the moment. They are a fairly cheap to buy, and can be sold to new startups looking for a catchy domain name. Zynga,

Google and Instagram were all catchy, brandable domains at one point.

Before you close this page and go to register thousands of brandable domains, I'd like to say that I've always found the brandable domain niche to be rather like a lottery. They are domain names that companies are not actively seeking. They're not domain names that could improve a brand's online presence, or help them with marketing campaigns.

There are, however, an increasing number of startups who are looking to domain marketplaces such as Brand Bucket to buy catchy startup domain names for a fairly small investment.

There are those who do very well out of this niche this DomainSherpa interviewee is one example: http://www.domainsherpa.com/mike-navarininamerific-interview/

Exact Match Domains

A sturdy niche, but declining in value thanks to Google. In the past, an exact match domain for a popular Google search meant that you essentially owned that niche. After many internal changes at Google, exact match domains are losing their power, and some consider them to be a thing of the past.

Many companies still see the value in exact match domains, and therefore may still buy them. They can also be a good form of lead generation in the right niche. I own a 3-word .COM domain name in a very competitive niche. Thanks largely to the exact match domain name I own; I have got the website into the top 5 search results on Google.

Keywords In General

Keyword domain names – nouns, verbs, places, activities, sports .COM keywords can all be solid investments, although as usual it's best to do plenty of research before buying a domain like this. Check out the searches per month, Google results and CPC to start with.

These are my recommendations as to which domains you could buy when entering the domain name industry, but at the end of the day it is down to you. Look at the various metrics:

- the TLD the age

- the number of competitors how many
- searches the domain receives per month
- the cost per click

Make sure you use all of this data along to make an informed decision before throwing your money away!

Know The Niche

Whatever you decide to buy, make sure you know the niche. That is extremely important. You should know whether there is a lot of online activity for that industry or not. If there is little online activity (no advertisers, company websites don't get updated often, no Facebook, LinkedIn or Twitter activity), then this should be a red flag.

My advice would be to know the niche that you are investing in. Research any niche thoroughly to know whether the user base is active online and whether they spend money online.

What to avoid

There are a two types of domain names that you should totally avoid when starting in the domaining industry. These are trademarks and typos, and both types of name can result in costly legal proceedings against you.

Trademarks

Stay away from any trademarked domain names completely. A trademark is a word or phrase which has been legally registered by a company. Trademarks are usually well policed, with many large firms employing their own trademark attorney. Their job is to find each and every trademark infringement, and taking action against those who infringe the trademarks.

Typos

Typos are common typographical errors or common misspellings of popular brands or companies. Typosquatters buy this type of domain to try to profit from the traffic in some way. Typo domains of popular brands such as oogle.com usually receive over 10,000 visitors per day.

What Price Should I Buy For?

What is your budget? How much money do you have available to invest? How many domain names do you want to invest in? These are all questions you should consider when trying to gauge your domain name budget.

I've mentioned a sale of mine in which I bought a domain name for $69 and sold it for $10,000. However, don't get hung up on the idea of buying $69 domains that no one else is bidding on. You may be able to flip these domain names every so often, but bidding on domain names in the $100+ range will generally give you a higher chance of selling your domains for four figures or over. This statement comes with a huge amount of caveats, and I'll explain later on more about how to choose the right domain to buy.

Chapter 4: Cybersquatting, Trademarks & UDRPs

The world of cybersquatting and trademark infringement may be new to you, but I believe that if you own a domain name you should be aware of the laws and regulations involved with online trademark infringement.

To the uninitiated, the ignorant or many journalists, domaining and cybersquatting go hand in hand. If you own a domain name but don't use it, they'd consider that as cybersquatting. There is such a thing as cybersquatting, but it is very different to domaining.

Domaining vs Cybersquatting

Domaining is investing in domain names. You buy a domain name in the hope of selling it on for a higher price, or by developing it to increase its value. In that sense, it is very much like investing in real estate.

True domain investors know very well that they should be avoiding certain types of domain names which contain trademarks, typos or copyrighted terms. As you're going to hopefully become a true domain investor, you'll know that you should avoid trademarks, typos and copyrighted terms. That's cybersquatting territory.

Cybersquatting is the practice of buying domain names which infringe on copyrights and trademarks. Cybersquatters will knowingly infringe on these trademarks in the hope of profiting from said infringement. This can be done by infringing the trademark completely (using the brand or company name outright), or by using a typo. Either way, this is something to avoid.

The arrival of new TLDs has – to some extent – made the problem of cybersquatting worse. I have seen many cases of new "domainers" registering trademarked new TLD terms in the hope that they will be bought by the trademark owner. This has resulted in many UDRPs being filed against individuals stupid enough to register trademarked terms.

Trademarks

Trademarks and intellectual property are recognizable signs and expressions of a particular product or service. They are used to claim exclusive ownership of the product or service. To use trademarks without licensing from the owner is an illegal trademark infringement.

Trademark infringement within domain names usually concerns unlawful use of a brand name to promote a website or product with no connection to the original trademark owner. This can be a big problem for large companies in particular. One example would be to register an Armani domain name to sell counterfeit Armani clothing.

To protect the interests of these large companies, many employ Intellectual Property Lawyers who will work solely on finding and removing trademark infringing domain names and websites.

The first step a company will usually take against a domain name is to send the owner a Cease and Desist letter either by email or postal mail. These letters usually demand that you transfer the domain name to them, and stop buying domain names which may infringe their trademark.

If you do get one of these letters, and you have absolutely no case (for example, you've registered a domain name with the word "Facebook" in it), then it is best to transfer the domain over. If on the other hand you believe that the company is wrong, and your domain doesn't infringe the trademark in any way, then may wish to consult with a domain name lawyer.

If a Cease & Desist letter doesn't work, then they may start legal proceedings against you, which usually results in a UDRP. This will be explained in a minute.

Before you consider buying a domain name, you may wish to check to see if there is an active trademark on the word or phrase. To do this, go to "www.uspto.gov" (for the USA) and enter the word or phrase. If there is an active trademark, stay well away.

It's also worth noting that if you are looking to invest in real estate domain names as many do, the term Realtor is trademarked and heavily protected, so stay away from any domain with the term Realtor in it. In fact, whilst researching UDRPs, I came across a UDRP for "austinrealtors.com", filed by the National Association of Realtors. As of writing this, the case is still active, but I assume that the domain name will be transferred over to the National Association of Realtors.

Typos

Typos, as explained earlier, are domain names which infringe on a trademark by counting on a users' typing errors whilst entering a web address. For example: a typo of DomainName.com may be DomainMame.com.

Typos can produce a lot of traffic, and potentially a lot of money for those who own the typos. A typo of Facebook.com – Fcebook.com received an estimated
92,400 visitors in January 2014. Unsurprisingly, Facebook now owns Fcebook.com. However, if it were privately owned, the registrant could earn thousands of dollars every month from the domain.

Many brands aggressively pursue typo-squatters, such as Facebook. In 2013 they were awarded $2.8million in damages from eleven people who registered typos of the Facebook domain name (for example, fnacebook.com and fmcebook.com).

Each of the eleven defendants in that case had to pay Facebook between $5,000 and $25,000 per domain name that they registered.

The moral of the story is: stay away from typo domain names.

UDRPs

UDRPs – Uniform Domain Dispute Resolution Policy is a process which aims to resolve disputes between trademark holders and domain name registrants. Usually, a UDRP is filed to recover domain names which are abusive (for example, MarkZuckerbergSucks.com), or which infringe a company's trademarks (for example, FacebookPage.com).

UDRPs are usually preferred by companies over lawsuits as they're quicker and far less expensive than a lawsuit. They are also mandatory, meaning that if you did receive a UDRP notification, you have no choice but to go along with it.

I could go into a lot of detail here about companies using a UDRP to try to essentially steal a domain name which they either can't afford or won't pay for (Reverse Domain Name Hijacking), but for the sake of this book, I'll be brief and simply say that a UDRP should be used for trademark holders to enforce their trademarks.

If you are sensible in your domain investments, you'll never receive a Cease & Desist letter or a UDRP notification.

Famous UDRPs

Madonna vs Madonna.com – in 2000, the singer Madonna filed a UDRP for the domain name Madonna.com. Madonna argued that she'd used the name as a brand since 1979, and wanted to receive ownership of Madonna.com. The domain name owner

– who was hosting sexually explicit content on the site

— had paid $20,000 for the domain name previously. Needless to say, Madonna ended up winning the ownership of Madonna.com.

The Estate of Jimi Hendrix vs JimiHendrix.com – the owner of JimiHendrix.com was, at the time, the owner of other domain names such as ElvisPresley.com and JethroTull.com. JimiHendrix.com was supposedly used as a fan club for Jimi Hendrix, but The Estate of Jimi Hendrix argued that the fan site was merely a front for trying to sell the domain name. JimiHendrix.com was awarded to The Estate of Jimi Hendrix.

Julia Roberts vs JuliaRoberts.com – This case was very interesting. The registrant – Russell Boyd was using JuliaRoberts.com as satire website about Julia Roberts the actress. Julia then filed a UDRP to get her domain name, which she won after finding that Boyd had put JuliaRoberts.com up for sale on eBay. After this result, Boyd then filed a lawsuit against Julia Roberts claiming she is "using her influence" to disrupt his use of the domain JuliaRoberts.com. The domain is now owned by Julia's lawyers.

WWE vs WorldWrestlingFederation.com – The first ever UDRP case was put forward by WWE against the owner of WorldWrestlingFederation.com. The UDRP panelist decided that WWE should own the domain name, as the "respondent has no rights or legitimate interests in the domain name".

Now that we've covered the basics of domain names and domain name law, we can start to learn about buying and selling domain names. In the next chapter I'll show you the tools which you will need to start domaining.

Chapter 5: Start Domaining

In this section, I'll be taking you through the methods involved in buying a domain name and selling it on for a profit. You won't be developing a domain name; you won't be creating landing pages or anything else. You'll be buying a domain and selling it for a profit.

However, I just want to say — it's not that easy. It's not a case of buying any domain name and expecting someone to pay thousands of dollars for it. That's gambling. This is investing.

Starting the right way

Before you start to buy and sell domain names, take a few hours to invest in yourself. That might sound strange, but I'm talking about your online web presence of course! Your own online web presence is very important, and can sometimes be the difference between a sale and no sale.

You should set up your own website, email address, email signature and social media accounts based around your domain names. Here's how and why:

Your Website and Domain Name

If you haven't already registered your own name as a domain name, go and do that now. This should be a .COM or your own country code domain name.

Once you've done that, I'd recommend that you set up a website. This should at least be a one-page website with your name and contact details on it, but if you'd like to set up something more complex and have the time to do so, then by all means do.

This is done just in case a prospective buyer decides to look you up online to make sure that you are a legitimate domain name seller that they can trust.

Your Email Address

When you're sending a professional email to someone, you want to come across as a trustworthy, established business person. Would you buy a domain name from someone who uses the email address TruPlaya4Life@email.com? No, didn't think so.

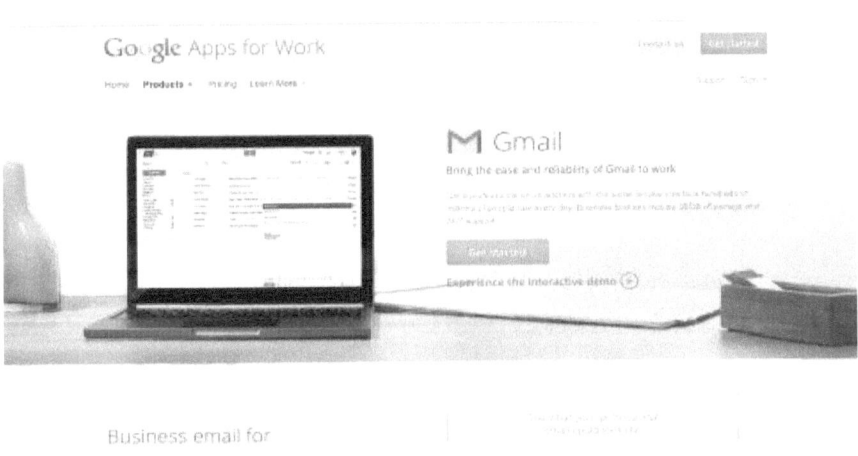

Take a few minutes to set up a professional email address. Most hosting companies will give you a free email account with your hosting account, but I prefer to use Google Mail within their Google Apps for Work setup. (https://www.google.com/work/apps/business/)

This lets you set up a personalized domain name for Google Mail quite easily. It's cheap to set up and there are plenty of tutorials available online to show you exactly how to set up your account. I'll be introducing you to a couple of very useful Google Mail plugins later on in this book, so it would be a good idea to set up your Google Mail account before then.

Your Signature

Adding a signature to each email you send out to sales leads will ensure that your prospective buyer is aware that you are authoritative and legitimate. You should include your name, title, phone number and website address at the very least. For example:

John Doe

CEO John Doe Domain Group

Phone: 1-888-888-8888

Website: www.johnsmith.com

To ensure that you comply with the CAN-SPAM act, you should also include a valid postal address within your email.

Social Media

It's a good idea to either set up a LinkedIn page if you haven't already done so. LinkedIn pages usually rank highly for Google name searches, so if a prospective buyer does Google you, they'll be able to see your fully branded LinkedIn page.

You may also use LinkedIn to connect to other members of the domain industry. I've made some very useful connections to people in domain related companies that would never have been possible without the use of LinkedIn.

Where to start

We are finally going to talk about how you can get started in buying domain names. I'd warn anyone who's new to the domain industry to be cautious at first. Don't buy/bid on names that you can't afford, don't buy hundreds of domain names and don't register brand new domain names. Just read, research and repeat.

Expired Domains

I'd recommend starting by looking at expired domain names. If you read the explanation of expired domains from earlier in this book, you'll know that these are domain names that have already been registered, but that registration has lapsed, meaning anyone can now buy the rights to the domain name.

In a typical domain lifecycle, the domain name would expire, be deleted and then be available for anyone to register. However, this hardly ever happens with domain names of any value. There are many services who catch domain names just as they expire and then auction those names off. This is where I'd recommend starting.

There are four companies who catch the majority of expired domain names: GoDaddy, NameJet, Pool.com and SnapNames.

GoDaddy will auction off expired domain names which have been registered to GoDaddy only. The other three services will catch domain names from a number of different registrars.

Prices for expired domain names vary:

At GoDaddy, their "Closeout" domains can be bought for as little as $5 (plus registration costs).

GoDaddy auctions have a minimum bid of $12. At NameJet, Pool and SnapNames, the current minimum backorder bids are $69 for a Pre-Release domain name and $59 for a Pending Delete domain name.

Many of the most popular names on NameJet and SnapNames in particular are backordered by more than one person, meaning that they then enter a private auction. Depending on the domain name and the amount of bidders, these names can go for thousands of dollars apiece.

After becoming successful at spotting expired domain names with some value, you may be interested in starting to acquire domain names privately – approaching the owner directly to make an offer. For now, expired domains will be a good way to learn about buying and selling domain names.

We shall cover the art of buying and selling expired domain names in a later chapter. For now, there are a few very important things to learn.

Tools you need to start domaining

To effectively invest in domain names, you'll need to use a number of tools and websites to find, maintain and sell your domain investments. It's entirely up to you as to which websites and tools you use. I'll simply list the domain related tools and websites that I believe are useful to any domaining workflow.

Expired Domain Search

Finding expired domain names is a big part of my domain investing strategy, and I look through thousands of domain names every day. The best tool I've used for finding expired domain names to buy is ExpiredDomains.net. It's a free to use website which has a comprehensive amount of filters, allowing you to search through GoDaddy, NameJet, SnapNames, Flippa and Sedo listings with relative ease.

I've used premium services such as FreshDrop.com in the past, but when you have a free service which is as good as ExpiredDomains.net, I fail to see why you'd pay for any other service. I can't fault ExpiredDomains.net. They even send me an email every morning with my daily domain list.

Drop Catching Services

As I mentioned previously, expired domain names are a large part of my domaining strategy, and as such, drop catching services are vital. The three drop catchers I use are: NameJet, SnapNames, GoDaddy and Pool.com. These seem to cover the vast majority of registrars and the best domain names. I'd recommend signing up for accounts at:

1. auctions.godaddy.com – an annual subscription of $4.99

2. www.namejet.com – a free service

3. www.snapnames.com – a free service

4. www.pool.com – a free service

Domain Name Parking

Domain name parking allows you to display adverts on your domains without having to develop them out with original content and articles. When you have a number of domains to manage, you may wish to use a domain parking service for a couple of reasons:

1. Receive residual income from your domain names via PPC advertising

2. A tool to attract domain sales leads. Some domain parking companies allow you to show a banner stating that your domain is for sale. This simple message can attract many leads.

Although domain parking as an industry is declining – with many services such as
Parked.com closing down recently, it's still a popular way to manage your domain names.

I've used a few domain parking services in the past: Bodis.com, Sedo.com, Parked.com, WhyPark.com and Voodoo.com to name but a few.

However, there is now only one parking service that I'd use: InternetTraffic.com. It's a service which is owned by domainer Frank Schilling's company

DomainNameSales.com. In my opinion, the platform provides the highest returns in terms of PPC revenue. The parked pages are also well designed, and the "for sale" banner is well positioned and highly visible.

The other advantage of using InternetTraffic.com is the fact that it's integrated with DomainNameSales.com's brokerage website, giving you access to a state of the art domain sales management portal. It also allows you to use DomainNameSales.com's domain brokers to help you to sell your domains.

You can sign up now for a free account at www.domainnamesales.com

Domain Sales Accounts

To ensure that your domain names receive maximum exposure to potential buyers, you may want to add your domains to a number of websites. The websites I recommend are:

- GoDaddy.com's Premium Listing Service (30% commission) – using GoDaddy's Premium Listing Service enables your domains to be shown in GoDaddy user searches.

- Afternic.com (20% commission) – their DLS promotion system allows your name to be shown across multiple registrars such as eNom.com and Moniker.com.

- DomainNameSales.com (10% commission) – their brokerage system as well as their partnership with DomainTools.com makes listing with DomainNameSales.com a must.

- Sedo.com (15% commission) – one of the largest domain marketplaces, with millions of dollars of sales per week.

WhoIs Tools

Using WhoIs data is vital for selling domain names. I use WhoIs data at least ten times every single day to find prospective domain buyers and to find out who owns certain domains I'm interested in buying. There are two tools that I use which are:

- **DomainTools.com:** Create a free account at DomainTools.com to start using their services. Their WhoIs listings show everything you need to know about any domain name including the registrant's email address and vital domain details such as creation and expiry dates.

- **Whoisology.com:** This is a service that I've recently started to use which lets you see all of the domain names owned by a single person or company. This data can be used effectively when trying to sell your domain names. Or simply if you want to spy on someone's purchases!

Sales History

Having the knowledge of previous domain name sales can help you to price your own domain names, and it may help to shape your future investments. Sales history can determine how much you're willing to spend on a domain name, and how much you can
realistically sell it for. There's a very useful website called NameBio.com which keeps a historical record of domain sales.

Plug any keyword into **NameBio.com**'s search engine and it'll show you domain sales from all the major marketplaces and websites.

An alternative website is **DNSalePrice.com**, but from my research this doesn't seem to have been updated for over a year. But still, the historical data is accurate.

DNJournal.com is also one of the best resources for domain name sales data. Ron Jackson, the editor of DNJournal, posts a weekly domain name sales table. It's always an interesting read, and can really help to gauge your own selling prices.

Email Tools

There are two tools that I use which have become vital to my domain sales strategy: Boomerang and Sidekick. Both are free (although there are optional upgrades), and both are extremely useful to own.

If you have a Gmail account, or use the Gmail for business platform, then I'd recommend adding these two plugins now. If you haven't got Gmail, then might I suggest registering a Gmail account for your domain sales. It's the best email platform I've used.

 BOOMERANG FOR GMail

Boomerang for Gmail

When sending domain sales emails, there are certain times of the day/week which work better than others in terms of responses. I've always found Tuesday & Wednesday midmorning to be a great time to send emails, and have had good response rates at those times. However, what if you can't send emails at those times? What if you only have an hour in the evening in which to find prospective buyers?

Boomerang will help you there. You can now write your emails at any time of the day or

night, and schedule them to send at a specific time. All you need to do is install Boomerang, and click on the "Send Later" button when composing your emails.

There is another feature that allows you to send a follow-up email to your prospective buyers if you don't hear back from them. However, I don't like to bug people too much, and believe that if they haven't replied to the first email, then they aren't really interested. So, I don't usually use this feature.

You can download Boomerang for Gmail for free from www.boomeranggmail.com

Sidekick by Hubspot

Sidekick is one of the most valuable free tools that I use. It's essentially a plugin which allows you to monitor when a prospective buyer opens your email.

To use Sidekick for Gmail, you'll need to go to www.getsidekick.com and follow the signup procedure. Once you've done that, you can start to use Sidekick to its full potential.

On your next email you send – whatever it is, click on the 'Track email with Sidekick' button to test it out. The moment your email is opened, you'll get a notification telling you details such as where it was opened (their location), and which device they used to open it (mobile or PC).

It is a useful tool for domain sales emails because it can accurately show the open rate of your emails – do most of your emails get opened by their targets, or are they simply deleted without being read? This will go some way to telling you that.

Another very useful feature is that Sidekick tells you every time an email is opened – whether the same email is opened once or several times. Domain sales emails that are opened more than once mean one of two things:

1. The email has been forwarded to other members of staff to decide whether to buy the domain name or not
2. The email recipient is interested in the domain name and is opening your email again after researching you and the domain name further.

Either way, when a domain sales letter is opened more than once, it's often a good sign that they're interested.

You wouldn't necessarily know this without a powerful tool like Sidekick.

Domain Registrars

Every domain investor has their preferred domain name registrar which they use for a number of reasons – it could be the price, the customer service or the security they offer to safeguard your domain names. I have two preferences when it comes to domain name registrars: **Uniregistry** and **GoDaddy**.

Uniregistry is a fairly new domain name registrar, owned by domain investor Frank Schilling. His company has created a wonderful user interface and a system that makes it so easy to administer your domain names. I've transferred my most valuable domain names to their service, and I'll be transferring more there soon.

The reason that Uniregistry is such a good registrar for domain investors is that, as you read above, it was created by a domain investor. Therefore, everything is exactly where you'd expect it to be from a domain investors point of view. Every common action (such as name-server management) is easy to find and easy to change. If you're looking for a new registrar, choose Uniregistry.

When I started domain investing, Uniregistry didn't exist. I chose GoDaddy because of their pricing and their domain management system which makes it easy to manage any domain portfolio – small or large. They also offer a cheap hosting solution, which if you're looking to create websites may be of interest to you. Many of my domain names are still with GoDaddy, but I plan on moving to Uniregistry outright.

I'd like to make two recommendations of registrars to avoid, too. The first is 1&1. One of my first domain names was registered at 1&1, and I would never use them again. Their management system is confusing, their customer service is almost nonexistent and to cap it all, they threatened me with legal action over "an unpaid bill" - from a service which I cancelled months before. I ended up having to pay the money (only $150), as this was the only way they'd leave me alone.

The second registrar to avoid is Moniker. Up until a year or two ago, Moniker was a domain registrar of choice for many people. That was until internal changes at Moniker gave customers security problems, missing domain names, wrong WhoIs data and other problems.

As a result, a mass exodus of Moniker started. Customers have moved domain names away from Moniker at an alarming rate, losing at least 17,500 domain names per month since June 2014.

Estibot

Estibot is a free to use service with premium features available at a monthly cost. Estibot – by its own definition, estimates the price of a domain name. It uses factors such as sales history, CPC and the TLD to determine a recommended price. This is only a computer generated appraisal based on metrics, but an Estibot appraisal along with the other premium tools available there can help you to determine prices to buy and sell domains at.

I've recently started to use their array of premium tools, and I must say I'm impressed by how effective the tools are, and how much time they save me every day. I am paying $49 per month for the service, and have used their extensive range of tools to analyze thousands of domain names and find leads for domains I'm looking to sell.

You can sign up for an Estibot account here *(affiliate link)*

Payment

Of course, you'll want to know the best way to get the money that you make from every domain name sale. I only have two recommendations here: Escrow.com and PayPal.

Escrow.com

If you are going to sell a domain name for more than a couple of hundred dollars, then it's advisable to start using a third party to ensure that the transaction is secure and safe. That's where Escrow.com comes in.

Escrow.com President Brandon Abbey and his team have managed hundreds of millions of dollars' worth of domain name transactions. They work with companies such as eBay, GoDaddy and DomainNameSales.com on a regular basis, too.

If you haven't got a free Escrow.com account now, I'd recommend signing up for one.

Not every domain buyer that you deal with will have heard of Escrow.com, so it would be a good idea to introduce the Escrow.com service to your buyer with facts such as:

1. They provide Internet escrow services for domain names
2. They routinely work with companies such as GoDaddy, eBay and AutoTrader
3. They have a partnership with the United States Department of Commerce
4. They have provided escrow services for over $1billion of online transactions

PayPal

PayPal is the alternative domain sales payment system that I'd recommend. PayPal is excellent for small domain name transactions due to the fact that PayPal only takes a 4% cut of the sales price. However, I'd never trust PayPal for larger sales, as there are too many risks and too many things that could go wrong.

If you don't feel comfortable with using PayPal at all with domain name transactions, then stick to Escrow.com – it'll mean higher fees, but far more security.

If you haven't set up a PayPal account yet, go to www.paypal.com to set one up. A personal PayPal account will suffice for now.

Domain Related Websites

There are a few domain name websites and blogs which I'd recommend using on a daily basis to make sure you keep up to date with any important news within the domaining community.

Firstly, Domaining.com – a news aggregator showing the latest blog posts from various industry websites. It's interesting to visit this site at least once a day to browse through the domain name news. They also provide a daily newsletter.

DNJournal.com is a must-read website for anyone involved in domain names. I mentioned Ron Jackson and his DNJournal website earlier, but I'll mention him again here as his site really is indispensable to the domain name industry. It's largely thanks to his website that some domain name sales get recognized in national or international media, which in turn helps more people to get to know the world of buying and selling domains.

DomainInvesting.com is run by Elliot Silver, a domain name investor who always posts invaluable advice to his thousands of readers. From what I've read, he largely relies on flipping domain names to bring in income, and he does this very well. I personally read every article he writes, as he has a lot of wisdom to share with us!

TheDomains.com is run by Mike Berkens, a domain investor who owns around 75,000 domain names and routinely sells domains for hundreds of thousands of dollars. He produces a lot of articles about the legal side of domaining, including many interesting UDRP cases.

DomainSherpa.com is a wonderful resource for the domain industry. Michael Cyger, the owner of DomainSherpa.com, regularly interviews successful domain investors and business owners who see the value in a good domain name. His shows are always fascinating to watch. You'll learn a lot by watching the videos there.

Now that you have all the knowledge and tools in place to buy and sell domain names, we'll start to look at how to buy domains, where to buy them and what type of domain name you may want to buy.

I'd like to point out that this is only my point of view, and my methods. This may not necessarily work for everyone, and it may not work the first time you try it. However, I believe that this is a solid way to start investing in domain names.

Chapter 6: Acquiring Domain Names

Registering New Domain Names

Registering new domain names with the hope of selling them for a profit can seem like a good strategy; you only pay a few dollars per domain names, and if you sell one name that would cover the cost of every other name you've bought.

There are a few investors that do this well, and can make a lot of money from new registrations. I wouldn't advise this as a general strategy, though. The domain investors making money from new registrations are extremely experienced and know exactly which new registrations will sell and which won't. Many also register hundreds of new registrations in the hope of selling one for a large amount (which would cover their registration fees and more).

However, at this point in time, there are over 100 million .COM domain names registered, which should tell you one thing: 99% of domain names of value have already been registered. Of course, you can still register .COM domain names – but will anyone want those names? Probably not. As for that 1%, I'd leave that to those investors that I mentioned above.

I'd recommend that you start to look for domain names that are expiring. If you read my explanation of the domain name lifecycle earlier on, you'll know that expired domain names have lapsed in registration and are going to be available to register again soon.

Drop catching services – such as NameJet and SnapNames – work with registrars to "catch" these domain names just as the registration lapses, and they'll allow you to buy those domain names for a fee – usually starting at $69 for "Pre-Release Domains" and $59 for "Pending Delete" domains.

Buying Expired Domains

Be warned: you'll be spending your time looking through hundreds, if not thousands of domain names every day.

The ExpiredDomains.net filter panel. Navigate here to start building your filters.

To spot domain names that are worthy of your investment, you'll need to search through expired domain names. Every day, there are roughly 100,000 domain names that enter the "Pending Delete" stage, 40,000 GoDaddy auctions, 15,000 NameJet Pre Release domains and 10,000 SnapNames exclusive domains.

How will you search through these hundreds of thousands of names to find the right domain names, whilst keeping your sanity? Let me introduce you to ExpiredDomains.net. ExpiredDomains.net is a free to use website that allows you to filter out most of the junk domains, allowing you to view the domain names which you may just be able to profit from. Instead of looking through 180,000 domain names per day, you may be looking through 2,000.

At this point, go to www.expireddomains.net to set up an account and some filters. Here's what you need to do:

1. Register for free at ExpiredDomains.net
2. Set up your first filter by going to Marketplace Domains → Show Filter
3. Here, you can play around with various filters. These filters reduce the amount of domain names you need to look through by introducing parameters such as "No Hyphens"

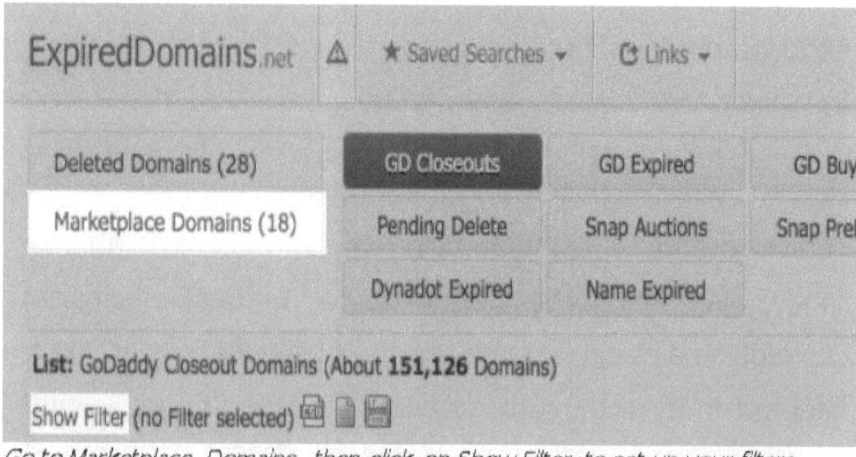

Go to Marketplace Domains, then click on Show Filter to set up your filters.

I won't be going into detail about the more advanced filters and settings of ExpiredDomains.net, but as a starting point, you'll want to use the following filters:

- No Numbers – no domains with numbers will be shown (this is to avoid domains such as 1domain0.com. If you want to search for numerical domains only, check "No Characters" instead)

- No Hyphens – no hyphenated domains will appear in searches

- Min WBY – using this will ensure no brand-new domains will be shown. I use a setting of around 2005 in my filter, allowing me to view domains which have been registered before 2005

- TLDs - .COM only, as we want to search for .COM domains.

- TLDs Registered – select .COM .NET and .ORG.
  This shows domain names which are registered in .COM, .NET and .ORG TLDs. Using this setting means one thing: there is at least some interest in those domain names, because other TLDs are taken.

- Name Ending – select either "ending today" or "ending tomorrow" to show domains which are ending soon.

There's little point in viewing domain names which will be dropping in a week or two.

Once you've done this, click on Apply Filter and your results will appear! At this point, it would be a good idea to save this filter so that you don't have to enter
those parameters every time you log into ExpiredDomains.net.

If you've followed my step-by-step guide from above, you'll be on the GD Closeouts tab. Use the following tabs to find expired domains:

- GD Closeouts (GD stands for GoDaddy)
- GD Expired
- Pending Delete
- Snap PreRelease
- NJ PreRelease

The other tabs that are available – such as Sedo Auctions, NameJet Auctions, Flippa and Dynadot can be set up so that you can monitor domain name auctions and sales from other marketplaces.

Deleted Domains (28)	GD Closeouts	GD Expired	GD Buy Now	GD Make Offer	GD Featured	GD Traffic	GD Most Active	GD TDNAM
Marketplace Domains (18)	Pending Delete	Snap Auctions	Snap PreRelease	Sedo Auctions	Sedo Fixed	NJ PreRelease	NJ Auctions	Flippa
	Dynadot Expired	Name Expired						

List: GoDaddy Closeout Domains (About **238** Domains) | **Saved Search:** GoDaddy Closeout Domains (save)

Show Filter (5 Filter selected, Reset) 🔲 🔲 🔲   Page 1 of 2 | Next Page ▸

Domain	LR	PR	BL	DP	WBY	ABY	Alexa	Donor	C	N	O	B	I	D	BG	CO	CPC	Traffic	Valuation	Price	Listing Type	RL
wyomsporting.com	12		0	6	1996	1997	0	-							0	0	0.00 USD	0	0 USD	9 USD	Buy Now	
netyork.com	7		0	0	2003	1997	0	-							90	16	0.90 USD	0	0 USD	10 USD	Buy Now	
juniporonline.com	13		0	0	2003	1998	0	-							75	18	2.63 USD	7	0 USD	11 USD	Buy Now	
fritlweb.com	6		4	9	1958	1999	0	-							0	0	0.00 USD	7	0 USD	9 USD	Buy Now	
taxnoxandison.com	13		2	4	2004	1999	0	-							0	0	0.00 USD	11	0 USD	5 USD	Buy Now	
freetly.com	9		5	14	2001	1999	0	-							0	0	0.00 USD	26	0 USD	10 USD	Buy Now	
myeshop.com	7		0	1	2003	1999	0	-							140	0	0.00 USD	4	0 USD	10 USD	Buy Now	
weodmerchant.com	13		0	0	1999	2000	0	-							0	0	0.00 USD	0	0 USD	11 USD	Buy Now	
handfedbirds.com	12		4	3	2003	2000	0	-							40	25	0.00 USD	0	0 USD	5 USD	Buy Now	
mailmesamples.com	13		0	0	2000	2001	0	-							0	0	0.00 USD	2	0 USD	9 USD	Buy Now	
vacationfavorites.com	17		0	0	2002	2001	0	-							10	64	2.43 USD	0	0 USD	10 USD	Buy Now	
greeklawyersonline.com	18		0	0	2003	2001	0	-							10	88	0.37 USD	0	0 USD	10 USD	Buy Now	
mywetschick.com	10		1	0	2006	2001	0	-							0	0	0.00 USD	4	0 USD	8 USD	Buy Now	
ultraadult.com	10		0	9	1998	2001	0	-							10	30	0.35 USD	0	0 USD	5 USD	Buy Now	
walkerwebs.com	10		0	6	2002	2001	0	-							0	0	0.00 USD	0	0 USD	5 USD	Buy Now	
clinicwork.com	10		1	0	2000	2001	0	-							20	10	0.00 USD	0	0 USD	3 USD	Buy Now	
thepussyclub.com	17		0	0	2003	2001	0	-							50	1	0.00 USD	2	0 USD	5 USD	Buy Now	
faithnchristchurch.com	19		0	0	2005	2001	0	-							0	0	0.00 USD	4	0 USD	5 USD	Buy Now	

A typical page of results after you've applied a filter.

Looking through pages and pages of domain names may take you a long time at first, but stick with it and soon you'll be able to read through thousands of domain names in no time at all. When you've found a domain name that you might be interested in, stop your search, open a new browser window and do some research on that domain to see if it's worthy of investment.

On the day of writing, I used this exact filter to find domains such as enhancedlife.com, marketindicators.com, newlookdental.com, gameshare.com and pcassist.com, so this setting will produce a lot of excellent domains which are available to backorder.

Go through each tab that I recommended above to search for domain names from GoDaddy, NameJet and SnapNames.

How to spot the good domains

Now that you've got your list of domain names, you'll want to find domain names that are suitable to backorder or buy. Going through each domain using a Yes/No system asking yourself questions about each domain can quickly eliminate domains.

Consider the following questions:

- **Is it a trademark or a typo?** If yes, discard immediately
- **Does is make sense?** If it doesn't make sense, discard immediately
- **Does it pass the radio test?** (would a potential customer be able to navigate to the domain after hearing it in a commercial?). If doesn't pass the radio test, discard.
- **Are there end users for the domain name?** - Are there companies to sell the domain name to? It may be that they use the phrase in their adverts, or use a similar domain name. Google search for an idea of how many

companies would be buy the domain name if you bought it.

> If there are no end users – or very few end users, discard the name.

Once you've further refined your list to remove the domains that don't pass the tests above, you'll have a few domain names that you might be interested in buying. At this point, it's good to do some real research before placing a bid. You may find that after researching the domain name, you will want to steer clear of it.

Use the following tools and websites to find out everything there is to know about the name and its competitors:

- **Screenshots.com & Archive.org** – see whether the domain name was ever used by another company. This search may show that your domain has a history of questionable use and content. I'd steer clear of any domain with a questionable history
  (such as spam, porn or illegal activity)

- **CheckPagerank.net** – does the domain name have a negative PageRank? If so, avoid it as it will have a checkered history.

- **Google Index** – is the domain name indexed on Google? It's interesting to find out whether the domain has a search engine history. Go to Google.com and type in *site: [yourdomain.com]* to find out whether any pages are indexed

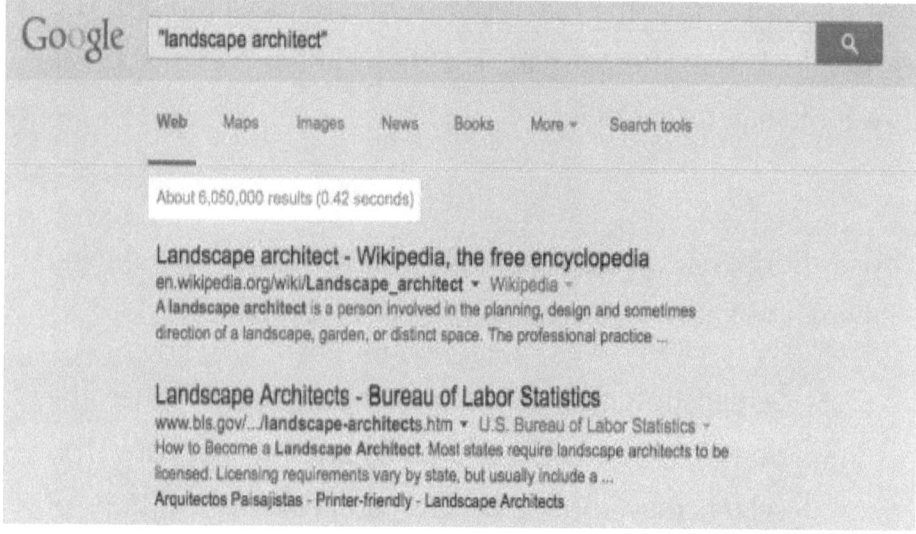

- **"Exact" Search on Google** – how many pages are indexed for the domain phrase?

I'll take an example of one of my domain names: LandscapeArchitect.com (above). To find out how many pages are indexed for the term, I'd type in *"landscape architect"* (including the quotation marks). It shows 6 million results, meaning that a lot of websites use the term. This is a positive. The more pages that show up under an exact Google search, the better as it shows that there are plenty of people who are using

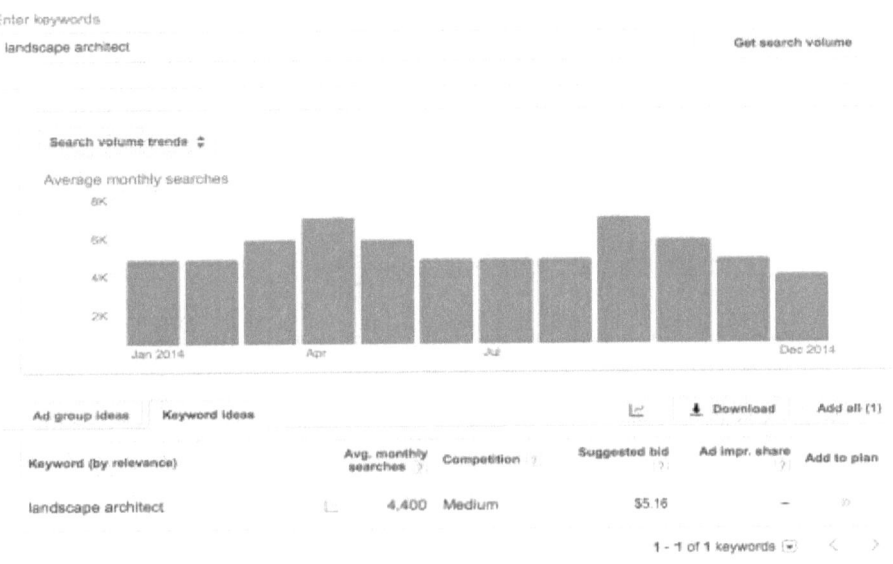

that exact phrase, whether it's just in the content on their website or in their page titles.

- **CPC – Cost Per Click:** This is the amount of money someone will pay for advertising on a search term.

To find out this number, go to "https://www.adwords.google.com/KeywordPlann"– Google's Keyword Planner and type in your phrase. To take the example of *landscape architect* again, the CPC is $5.16, and the competition is Medium. Meaning there are companies actively advertising on the keyword.

- **SpyFu.com** – This is a neat website which I've used for a while. It enables you to see who is advertising on a specific keyword, and what their rough ad spend is. If a company is advertising on a keyword or phrase that you own, then they may be more likely to buy the name from you.

  There is a paid option with SpyFu, but for now you can see a few results without having to pay. If it's something that you find useful, then you may consider paying their monthly membership in the future.

- **Estibot**: If you've registered for an Estibot account, you may be interested in knowing that much of this data can be gained by appraising each domain name with Estibot.com. To research a domain name at Estibot, use the following steps:

  1. Enter your domain name in the Appraise box on the Estibot.com homepage, then click on the "Appraise" button.

2. This will send you to a page detailing your domain name's appraisal price, the keywords, monthly searches, CPC, related domain sales and the registration status of other major TLDs.

3. If you have an Intermediate, Advanced or Expert Estibot account (if you pay $49.95 or more per month), then click on "Help Me Sell This Domain".

4. Click on the "Generate Leads" button at the bottom of the page and Estibot will generate a report for you based on websites that Estibot thinks may be interested in the domain name.

5. The more leads that are produced in this report, the better. If a domain you want to buy only has say 10 leads, I'd avoid it as the chances of selling the domain are quite low.

The data from Estibot can help to form a decision on whether or not you want to buy the domain name.

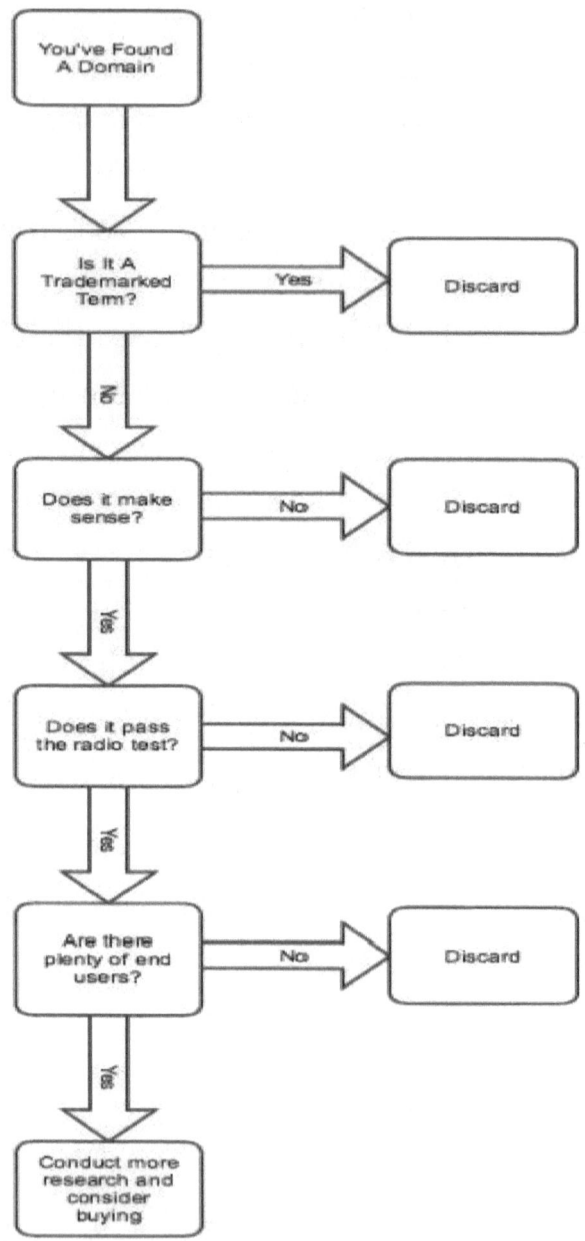

Once you've decided that you're interested in placing a bid for your domain name, you'll need to be organized and a little bit sneaky in order to get the domain for a good price. You see, there are many users who check the auction closing-soon section to see which domain names have bids.

If you've found a domain name that has 0 bids, and you don't want to attract too much attention to the fact that you've found that great domain, then consider placing your backorder/bid just before the deadline.

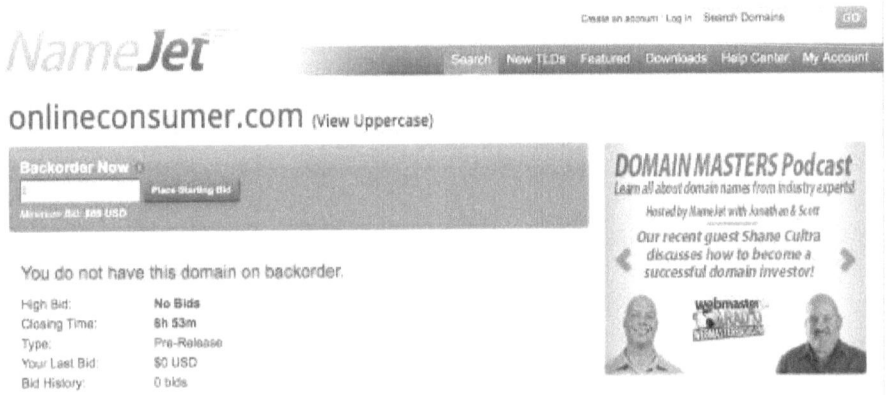

Let's take an example of a domain name I've found today: OnlineConsumer.com. Here are some quick facts to see why I like the name:

1. It's registered in 1998 – I do like to own older domain names

2. The .Net and .Org are registered
3. There are 484,000 results for an exact search for "Online Consumer"
4. It passes the radio test
5. There are no trademarks to consider

No one has placed a bid on the domain so far, and there is 8hrs 53mins until the deadline to backorder the domain. Just in case someone sees this domain, I will set a timer for 8hrs 48mins. This gives me 5 minutes to backorder this domain name. It also gives me the best possible opportunity to acquire the domain for $69.

Whatever we can save on costs here is more profit later on down the line.

If you're using NameJet, Pool.com or SnapNames to backorder a domain name, then there are two possibilities which can occur after the backorder deadline has passed:

1. The domain name enters an auction, because more than one person has backordered the domain name. This will be an auction will usually last three days. If this

happens, you'll be notified by email of the auction end date. Be sure to set a reminder to visit the auction in the hour before it closes.

2. The domain name backorder has been successful and you now own the domain name. The funds will be automatically taken from your credit card or bank account, and you'll be notified within a couple of days as to where your domain name is now registered.

If A Domain Goes To Auction

As I said earlier, the more popular domain names will be backordered by more than one person and so it will be sent to an auction. Make a note of the time that the auction ends, set a reminder for an hour before the auction ends and then do nothing until then. You shouldn't enter into a bidding war before that final hour, otherwise you are likely to push the price up too much. Our whole aim here is to buy this domain name for the lowest amount possible.

Once you're into that final hour, keep monitoring the auction and see what the price is with 10 minutes left to go. It may be that there are a few other bidders who are determined to own the domain name, which will push it out of your budget range. If this happens, then just find another domain name.

Buying Domains

Looking to start buying domain names to flip for profit? Here's my handy infographic to help you out.

Look for domains

1

Use a website such as ExpiredDomains.net to start to find expired domain names that are worthy of investment.

Use filters to help get rid of domains that are worthless.

Research

Use Google, Keyword Planner, SpyFu and other tools to start to research a domain you may be interested in buying.

Are there any factors which are putting you off buying the domain name such as its history?

Are there enough end users?

2

Make your bid

3

When you've decided that the domain name is suitable to buy or bid on, then wait.

Wait until just a couple of minutes before any bidding deadline to make your bid. You're more likely to secure your domain name for less money this way.

Unless, of course it's a very popular domain in which tens if not hundreds of people will be bidding.

You've won!

Hopefully, you'll have won your backorder or auction. Did you win the domain name for a small fee? If so, even better.

Never overpay for a domain name. If you're unsure about prices, check historical sales figures to see how much that type of domain name is selling for at the moment.

You should always have a maximum bid in mind to ensure that you don't overpay for your domain.

If it goes above your maximum budget, move on to the next domain name.

4

In this case, you're likely to be outbid by those with deep pockets.

Park It

5

If you've bought the domain name to flip [sell quickly], then it would be a good idea to park the domain name at a service such as DomainNamesales.com for now.

111

If the price is within your budget with 10 minutes to go, then wait. Wait for a couple more minutes and then place a bid. Bids can be placed in increments of $10 to start with at NameJet (e.g $69, $79, $89), so consider placing a bid at $10 above the current price.

That bid may be enough to win the domain name. If it isn't, and another bidder places a higher bid, then consider your maximum bid and go to that price, and no higher. If a bid is placed within the last couple of minutes, then extra time is added on to ensure that all parties have a chance to place further bids.

A bidding war can be fun, but don't get carried away – stick to your budget. Don't be tempted to go higher than you are comfortable with purely to win the auction.

If you do win the auction, then the website (NameJet, SnapNames, Pool etc) will contact you once the payment has been processed.

How Much Should You Buy a Domain For?

A common question between domainers is: How much should I spend on a domain name? This is a difficult question which has seen many different answers from many different domain investors.

Some say that buying domain names on the aftermarket for thousands of dollars is ok if you can then flip the domain name to make one or two thousand dollars in profit. Some say to stick to various ratios on based on how much income you have, or how much money you have set aside for domain names.

If I were starting in domain names today, I would give myself a budget of around $250 and I would buy three domain names. $250 divided by thee is around $83. So within my budget, I could easily buy three $69 domain names from NameJet.

Once you have those domain names, you try to sell all three for at least $300 to $500 each. Out of those three domain names, assuming you have invested well, you should get at least one sale. Assuming the sale was at $500, you'll then keep $250 for yourself & the Government, and invest the other $250 in three more domain names.

This is a hypothetical situation, but the strategy is one that I try to stick to: invest 50% of your profits in another domain name. Soon enough, you'll be able to buy and sell purely from profits.

So, how much should you buy a domain name for? I'd say that you should buy a domain name for no more than 50% of your profits from domain name sales.

Using a strategy like this to start with minimizes the risk. It's worth remembering that $69 domain names will usually only get you to a certain level of income, and a fairly small return on investment. With the right domain names, you'll be able to turn a $69-$100 investment into hundreds, but rarely into thousands.

At some point you may start to become interested in the higher priced domain sales (four figures and higher), in which case a budget of $200 or higher per domain will probably be needed. As always though, do your research before spending hundreds or thousands of dollars on a domain name.

How do you know if a domain name is valuable?

To determine the value of any domain name – expired or otherwise, you have to look at data. There are very few who can successfully buy and sell domain names based on gut instinct. The values that I've shown you earlier in this book – the TLD, the CPC, the number of advertisers, the domain name's age and the number of Google searches per month.

These factors, along with sales history and current demand can tell you whether or not a domain name is valuable, and how valuable it is. A domain name with 10,000 exact searches on Google every month with a CPC of $8 is going to be far more valuable to an end user than a domain with 500 exact searches and a CPC of $1.

Use this data along with sales history and an Estibot valuation to determine the value of a domain. If you're buying a domain name for $69 that's got a $5,000 Estibot value, 1,000 searches per month and a CPC of $3, then you have a good deal.

You aren't going to find this quality of domain name every day, so patience is key. Save your money for a domain name that matches all of your criteria.

Owning the domain name

Once you've won your backorder/auction, you'll be sent an email telling you where your domain name is now registered. There is one thing that you must know about once you own the domain name, and that is auction lock.

Auction lock can be a real pain for those of us looking to flip domain names within a matter of weeks. The auction lock affects any domain name which is won at NameJet and registered at eNom.com, and once the domain name hits your eNom.com account, you may see the Auction Lock warning – telling you that you are unable to transfer the domain name for 42 days. This means selling the domain name will have to wait until that 42 day period is up. It's something that can't be changed.

Anyway, now that you own the name – whether you have auction lock or not, you'll need to do something with your domain name. You could find a buyer for the domain name, you could create a website and sell leads, or you could park the domain name and wait for buyers to come to you.

All three are plausible, and all three can bring success. Whatever you decide to do, I'd put it into park to start with to see how much traffic the domain name gets and how much revenue it produces.

If you're not sure about how to put your domain names into park, then follow these quick instructions:

1. Sign up for a parking account. For these instructions, I'll use DomainNameSales.com. I park all my domains with them.
2. Change the name servers of your domain name(s) to: buy.internettraffic.com and sell.internettraffic.com to ensure that your domains are pointing to DomainNameSales.com's platform. This is done in your registrar's domain management dashboard.

3. Visit http://www.domainnamesales.com/signup and fill out all of the details.

4. After your account has been approved, you can log in and go to www.domainnamesales.com/sales to see your domain dashboard.

5. Go to Domains → Add domains and add all the domain names you want to here.

6. They'll be reviewed to ensure that you do own the domains, then they'll appear in your Portfolio, and adverts will start to appear on the domain name.

A few tips for when you park domain names:

1. Don't whatever you do click your own ads in an effort to get yourself some extra revenue! This will probably get you banned from the parking service altogether.

2. Don't expect to receive a lot of revenue unless you own some high-end premium domain names. Most domain names may make just a few dollars every month. You can't count on parking revenue to fund your future domain purchases as you could in the past.

How Many Domain Names?

How many domain names will you find to invest in? There are thousands of domain names which drop every day, but there are only a couple of domain names which may be worth investing in. And although there are investment-worthy domain names available every day, it's all about picking the right ones at the right prices.

This may be a difficult practice if you're new to domaining, but there are a few simple rules that you should try to stick to, especially when starting out:

1. Start by buying just 1 or 2 domain names to see whether this system works for you
2. Don't go over your budget. Try, if you can, to get domain names for $100 or less to start with
3. Buying domain names every day is not something you need to do. I buy one to two domain names a week. I bid on around 10 per week.

Investing in too many domain names can be a downfall for any investor, as you have to remember those dreaded renewal fees which come 12 months down the line. Owning too many domain names may mean that you can't afford the renewal fees, and you'll have to drop domain names or sell them cheaply simply because you can't afford to keep them.

Keep your portfolios very small until you have your system and strategy worked out completely.

How long after I buy the domain name should I wait to sell it?

There really is nothing against you trying to sell the domain name the day after you buy it. I would personally wait a couple of days after parking the domain name. This allows me to take a look at whether the domain receives daily traffic, or starts making any parking revenue. These factors could help me to decide a selling price.

When you are flipping a domain name, you must take into account various transfer restrictions that registrars have. For example, an eNom.com domain name won via auction at NameJet may have an auction lock, meaning you can't transfer the domain name at all for 42 days.

Chapter 7: Selling domain names

Now that we have an idea of which domain names to buy and where to buy them, you'll want to know how to sell them. At the end of this section, I'll show you a real-life example of a domain name that I was able to successfully flip using the methods I set out below.

So, you have your domain name. Hopefully you've been through the "buying domain names" section above which outlines how to buy domain names and which domains you should be buying. If you have, you'll have a domain that fits the following criteria:

1. It's a .COM domain
2. The .NET and .ORG are registered and in use by other companies
3. Through research you've found companies who own similar domains, or use the phrase in their current domain name.

Domains that fit these criteria should be fairly easy to flip for a profit if you haven't overspent in acquiring them. You'll soon find out if you have.

The first thing we need to do in order to sell the domain name is to check that it isn't in auction lock. This only affects domain names registered with eNom.com which you've recently purchased from NameJet. If it is in auction lock, you'll see a notice similar to this when you log into your eNom.com domain management area:

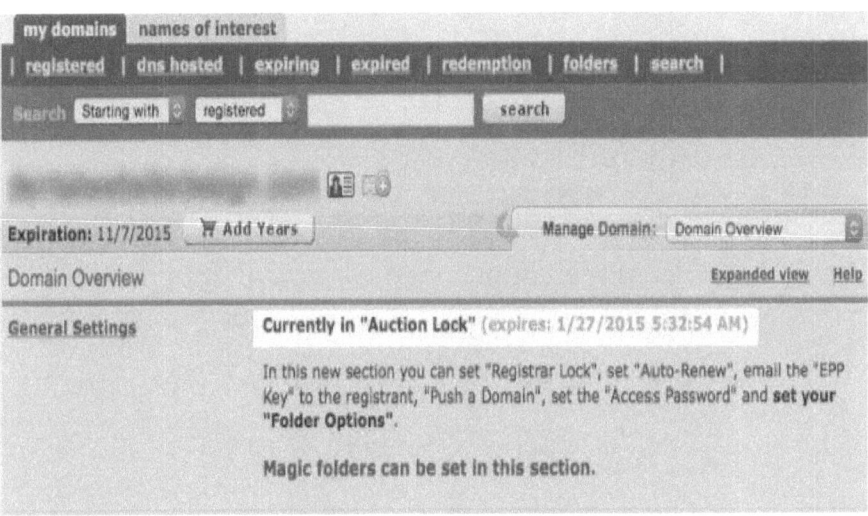

If it is in auction lock, just sit tight until the auction lock is lifted, as you won't be able to transfer the domain to your buyer whilst the name is in auction lock.

Once you've verified that you're OK to transfer your domain name to another person's account, you'll want to make sure that you have the following ready:

1. Open your Internet browser and go to Google.com
2. A DomainTools.com account (log into it now)
3. Whoisology.com open
4. Estibot.com (only if you have a paid account with access to the Lead Generation Tool)
5. A blank spreadsheet – if you don't have any spreadsheet software, you can use http://docs.google.com to create one
6. Your email account open. If you're going to use Boomerang and Sidekick (mentioned earlier), then you'll need to open your Gmail account in Chrome.

Then you can start looking for potential buyers. There are a number of places in which to do this. We're going to start with Google as they generally have the best data available to find leads.

Finding Leads

Google Leads

Go to Google and perform a search for the phrase or word contained in your domain name. As an example, let's take a domain name that I already own: DentalWebsiteDesign.com.

I chose to buy that domain name because:

- It was registered in 1998
- All other TLDs were registered and in use by competing companies
- The phrase is used by hundreds of websites (in their page titles, domain names and meta descriptions)
- Dental Website Design gets around 800 Google searches every month
- The CPC (cost per click) is high - $33.19
- There are plenty of companies advertising for my keywords I bought it for a good price

I'm not actively selling this domain name because I'm working with a company to provide lead generation services (explained later in this book). However, I will take you through the steps that I'd take to find qualified buyers for the domain name.

So, the first step I take in finding a buyer is to do a Google search for my keywords. In this case, it's *"Dental Website Design"*. Searching with the quotation marks ("") means that Google will only display web pages which use your exact keywords. In this case, Google is indicating that there are 198,000 pages which use the phrase "Dental Website Design". There are also 11 advertisers on the first page of results. That's a good sign, but we'll get to those advertisers later.

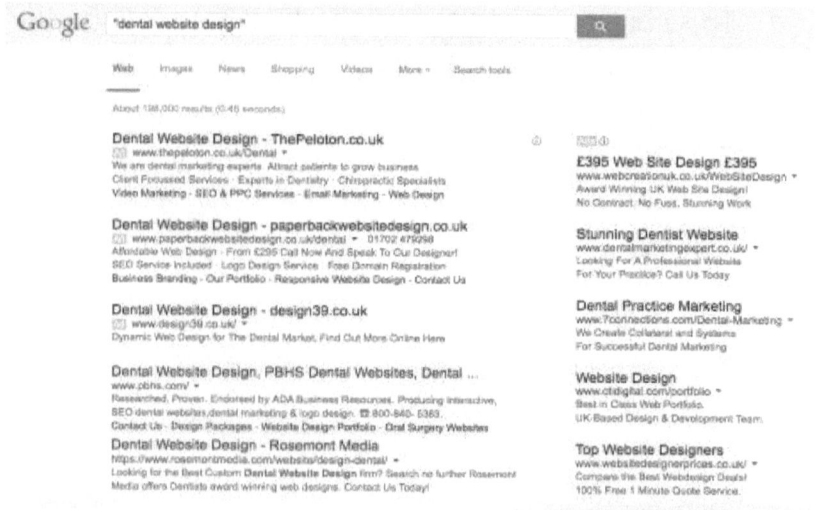

We're not going to be looking through 198,000 pages of results to find a buyer for our domain name. Chances are, the buyer of your domain name is listed within the first 3-5 pages of results. That's not a firm rule, but in general, your buyer will be listed within the first few pages of that search (this is true for domain names such as DentalWebsiteDesign.com, but may not be true for brandable domains, generic keywords or professional domains).

Open the first website that appears for your search. The key here is to take a look around their website and see what they offer and whether they would benefit from owning the domain name you're trying to sell.

In my case, with DentalWebsiteDesign.com, my first listing to visit is PBHS.com. From looking around their site, I can tell that they are the leaders in their market and they work closely with the American Dental Association. They also use the phrase "Dental Website Design" throughout their website, including in their page titles. They are obviously a company which understands technology and utilizes that technology. These are all good signs.

Once you've decided that this company is a good fit and would benefit from owning your domain name, you need to find the right person to contact. This is the most crucial part. Emailing the company's general contact email address is no good – the chances are that the company contact email address is monitored by lower level staff who'll simply delete your email. You need to find a specific person to contact in order to start a conversation.

If the company in question is a large company (50+ employees), you'll probably need to find the contact details for either the Director of Information
Technology or the Director of Marketing. The people in these positions are senior enough to make decisions about spending, or are in a position to take your proposition to the CEO or senior partners. Contacting a CEO or President directly is not something I'd normally do, as in general they'll have hundreds of unread emails in their accounts and very little time to read them all. This means that your sales letter will probably be deleted.

CTOs, Directors of Information Technology, VPs and Marketing directors are usually all good contacts. In a smaller company, or a sole trader setup, I've had the most success by emailing the owner of that company directly, as there generally isn't a person who's specifically in charge of online marketing or technology.

How do you find the right person to email? A combination of WhoIs, LinkedIn and Google.

WhoIs

WhoIs is a system that allows you to look up the owner of any domain name in existence. The most popular service is DomainTools.com – which is why I suggest that you sign up for an account with them (without an account, you're limited to 50 WhoIs lookups within a 24 hour period).

Firstly, do a WhoIs search for your company. In my Dental Website Design example, I did a WhoIs search for PBHS.com http://whois.domaintools.com/pbhs.com, and noticed that they use a general info@pbhs.com email for their WhoIs information. This is no good, as this email address is used by hundreds of their clients.

Our email will simply be deleted without reading.

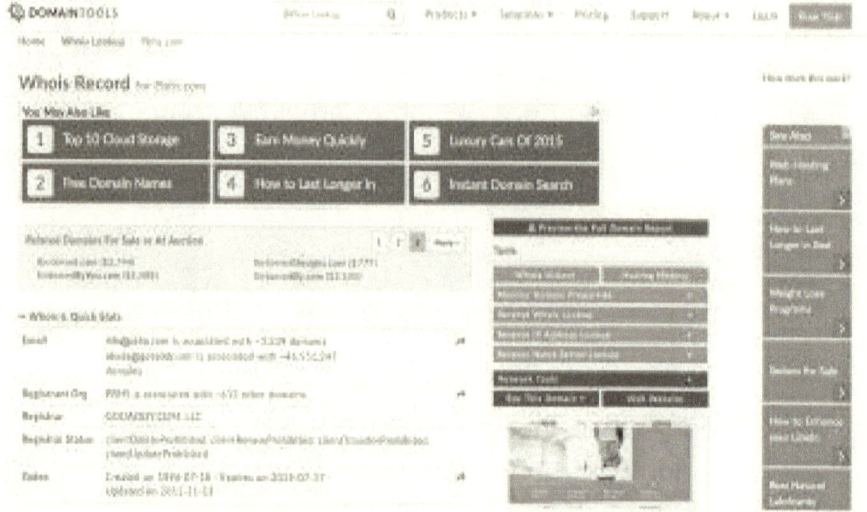

There are several scenarios in regards to contact details which can happen when you look up a domain name's WhoIs information:

1. The company uses a general information email (such as my example above). In which case, we won't use that email. We'll need to find another

2. An employee will be listed as the WhoIs registrant. If this happens, perform a Google search to find out who they are. *Hint: search for their name & the company name to find information.*

If they're not a decision maker (director, owner, vice president), then discard the email and do some more research.

3. The domain name is under privacy protection. This means that the company has hidden their details behind a proxy email. This email address shouldn't be used either.

4. The domain name is registered by a web designer a third party on behalf of the company. If this is the case, never email the designer or third party. You won't get anywhere with your domain sale by doing this.

If your WhoIs search didn't provide any decent results, we'll move onto the next method: LinkedIn

LinkedIn

The vast majority of major decision makers now have a LinkedIn page, and so it's fairly easy to find the right person to email. However, the way that LinkedIn is set up means that a lot of information isn't shown to free users, such as ourselves. So, we'll use Google to search through LinkedIn. All we need at this stage is their name. We don't need their email address just yet.

Here's what to do:

1. Go to Google.com
2. Type in: site:linkedin.com "at [your company]"
3. This means that Google will only show results from LinkedIn.com, and will show profiles that use the words "at [your company]" (obviously change [your company] for the name of the company you want to sell to.
4. If you want to refine this search further, you can do this: site:linkedin.com

   "director" "at [your company]". This will only show profiles that are listed as being a director at this company. *Hint: change "director" for "vice president" or "ceo" or "owner" - whichever person you want to find within an organization.*

5. Look through the results until you find the contact you need.

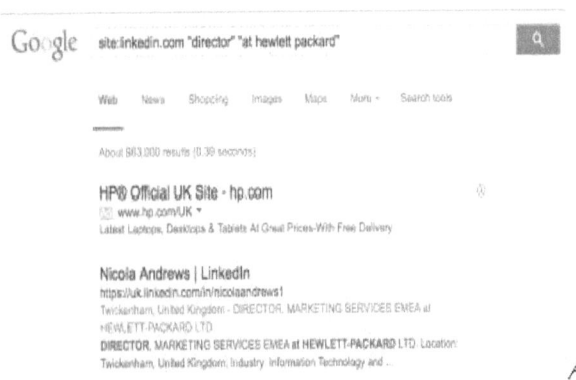

An example of the method explained above. In this case, I was looking for a contact at HP

I believe that LinkedIn is a tool which isn't used enough in domain name sales. This is the perfect way to incorporate a professional network into your domain sales strategy. This will work a lot of the time. However, there are occasions that you won't be able to find who you're looking for. If this is the case, you have a couple of options. A Google search or a search of their website. Let's go to a search of their website next. Remember, we're only looking for a name at this point.

Search Their Website

Many companies will add a "People" category to their website to introduce their website visitors to their staff. I'm not entirely sure what the point of this is — whether it's to make corporations appear more personable, I don't know. But it can be useful.

Generally, if the company includes a "People" or "Our Staff" section, they'll include the most important people within the company; Chairman, CEO, Vice
Presidents and
Directors. If the methods above haven't worked, browse through the company's website to see if a section like this exists. Then find the most appropriate person to contact. We only need their name at this stage, but if they list their email address too, then even better.

Some websites also include a blog in which some of their top executives contribute. I'm in the process of selling a domain name to Cisco Systems, and this is how I found the right person to contact there. Looking through their website can be profitable.

Google Search

If the methods above have failed, then return to Google to do a new search. Here, you're looking to find the name of your key contact within the company, so phrases such as "CEO at [your company]" or "Director of Technology at [your company]" may help you find their name.

You may be looking for anything from a news article or press release announcing a staffing change to a blog post which mentions their name.

Google usually has the right contact information if you look hard enough.

Getting the email address

Once you have the person's name, you obviously need their email address on which to contact them. I know there are some who prefer to phone a person directly to discuss a domain sale, but I've never done this. I don't particularly like speaking on the phone, and I've had good results from using email, so I'll continue with that.

If you've managed to get their email address using the methods above, then great! Move on to the next step. If not, don't worry. Corporate emails usually follow a simple pattern.

Most email addresses cover one of these formats. I'll use my John Doe as an example:

- john.doe@email.com

  (firstname.lastname@email.com)

- john@email.com

  (InitialLastName@email.com)

- johndoe@email.com

  (FirstNameLastName@email.com)

- j.doe@email.com

  (Initial.LastName@email.com)

- john@email.com

  (FirstName@email.com)

The chances are that if it's a larger company, their email address is pretty easy to guess. However, it's always useful to check, and that's where Google comes in (again).

A simple search for this: *email "@[domainname.com]"* will reveal a lot. (Change [domainname.com] for the company's domain name.) Looking through the results of a search like this will usually reveal the format of a company's email system. Somewhere amongst the results will be an email address. It doesn't necessarily need to be the email address of the person we're looking to contact, but at least we'll now know the structure.

Once you know the structure, you can guess the email address of the person you want to send to. Guessing alone isn't a good strategy, and it can lead to many emails not being received, so verify that the email address is correct. You can do this by going to a service such as www.verifyemailaddress.org or www.mailtester.com Here you can enter the email address you want to test.

The websites mentioned above allow you to enter any email address, and using several different methods – including pinging the SMTP email server, the websites can usually establish whether the email address exists or not.

If it comes back as being a real email address, then do the following:

- Open your spreadsheet
- Add their name in the first column
- Add their email address in the second column
- Add their current website in the third column

We want to keep all of our leads in one place, and a spreadsheet is the perfect space to do this in. Only once we've collected all of our leads will we start to email them.

Follow this method for other relevant websites and companies within your Google search. This can be time consuming, but it is worth it to send out relevant emails to real people within companies that may very well be interested in buying a domain name that you own.

Within the initial Google search which is mentioned above, you should be looking at website entries within the first three pages. In most circumstances, any company who is interested in ranking well for that term, or whose company name matches that search term will be ranked in the first three pages. That means looking through around 30 websites.

ZFBot Leads

Another excellent way to find a buyer for your domain name is to search for companies or individuals who own domain names which are similar to yours. This is where a website called ZFBot.com comes into play.

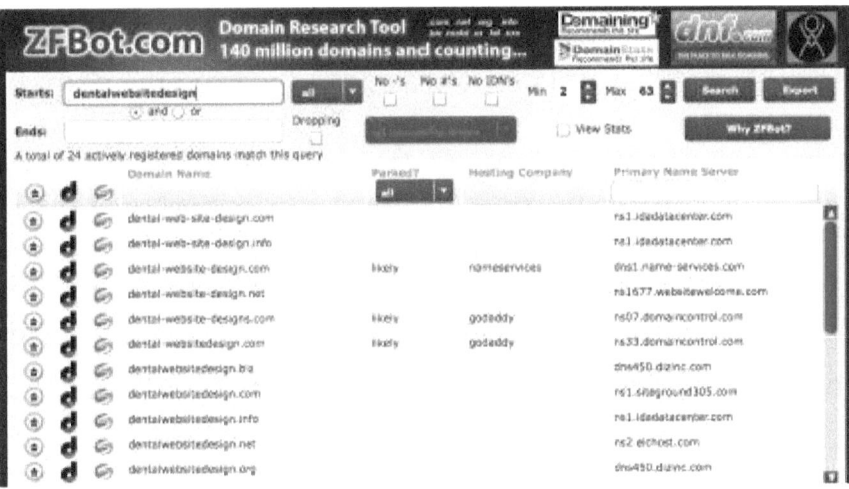

ZFBot allows you to search through the entire database of domain names for several gTLDs. You can search for domain names which start or end with your keyword. It also includes hyphenated domain names.

Searching for similar domain names to yours can be a very useful way of finding a buyer. Sometimes, a company owner will look to register a domain name, but will see that it's already registered. This means that they go with an inferior domain name – such as adding "llc" onto the end or using hyphens.

When you email them to notify them that the domain name is for sale, there may be a possibility (on condition of their budget) that they will be interested in upgrading the domain name.

This strategy is very useful for your keyword domain names which happen to also be a company name. An example would be a domain name I sold last year: EarlyDoors.com. I ended up using ZFBot to find a company using the domain name EarlyDoorsLtd.com.

Once you've found a company or individual who owns a similar domain name to yours, you'll need to go through the same steps as above in order to find out who to contact within that company.

These methods include:

- Using the WhoIs data
- Using a LinkedIn search
- Using a Google Search
- Searching their current website

Once you've found all the relevant leads from the ZFBot search, write the name, address and website in your spreadsheet to email later.

SpyFu Leads

A third valuable resource when finding domain name leads is to look on SpyFu.com to see who is advertising for your domain name's keywords.

I believe that anyone who is spending money on online advertising regularly is a possible candidate for buying a domain name. Why, you may ask? Well, they obviously have some idea of online technology and want to attract more visitors to improve their company's sales.

They're also not afraid to spend money online, and must be fairly active on the Internet in order to monitor and manage their adverts.

This is why I use SpyFu.com to search for potential buyers. Before I start to show you SpyFu.com, I want to let you know that you should only use SpyFu's data if your domain name keywords are:

1. Searched for every month (check using Google's Keyword Planner)

2. Have a CPC of over $1 (check using Google's Keyword Planner)

3. Have a medium to high competition rate (again, check using Google's Keyword Planner)

If your domain names don't meet one or more of these standards, then there's not much point in using SpyFu's data, as there are going to be very few, if any companies that you'll find via SpyFu.

I should also mention that whilst SpyFu does offer free data, a lot of the data is available to those with a subscription. Currently, that's $79 per month. I'm not telling you that you must or mustn't subscribe to SpyFu. That's entirely your decision. I'm purely listing SpyFu.com here as it's been useful to me in the past.

If your domain name meets the criteria above, then go to SpyFu.com and type in your domain name's keyword(s) in the Main search box at the top of the page. Once you press enter, you'll be shown an Overview box, telling you the keyword's statistics (although I believe that these statistics aren't as accurate as those in Google's Keyword Planner, especially the CPC).

If you scroll further down the page, you'll be met with such statistics as the number of advertisers within the last 3 months. Scrolling down further will show you a list of the most successful advertisers along with a monthly budget (again, I do not believe that the monthly budgets shown are anywhere near accurate).

As a free user you'll only have access to the top five advertisers. The rest are hidden and are only available with a premium subscription. The free data can give you some idea of who is spending money regularly on advertising for your keywords. You may be able to use this data to contact those advertising companies.

Scrolling down further will show you all of the ads currently running on Google for your keywords. Although this data doesn't show you specifics such as the amount of time they've been advertising for, or the total number of keywords they advertise for, it's still very useful data. It's also fully available to free users. Using this data could provide more qualified leads to sell your domain name to.

Selling your domain name to companies that advertise on your domain's keyword could be seen as a way of selling that company money. It will be worthwhile to include some statistics about advertising data within your domain sales email to them. I'll cover this in more detail in a subsequent chapter.

Social Media Leads

Do you have a Twitter or LinkedIn account? Using social media to sell your domain names can be profitable sometimes. I'll tell you about a personal encounter I had whilst selling a domain name for thousands of dollars.

I was attempting to find the right person to contact within a certain multi-national corporation who had just released a new product using a keyword/phrase which I happened to own. I tried for days to find the right person to contact within their corporation, and went through all of the steps that I listed above (WhoIs, Google Searches, LinkedIn Searches, Website Searches).

That's when I found an employee of this company on Twitter. After reading about them, I found out that they worked within the marketing department at their head office, so I hoped that they would be able to help me. They did.

Within an hour of me sending a Tweet (which I've since deleted), they had replied. Then, via Direct Message they let me know the person to contact within the company who was in charge of this new product.

I immediately sent this person an email and within a couple of days we had reached an agreement, and shortly afterwards the domain name was sold.

Using social media – especially Twitter and LinkedIn can be a useful way of making contact with a company representative when you have no other way of finding out information about the company and who to contact.

This is the only time I've ever needed to use social media to sell a domain name.

Estibot Leads

I have started to use Estibot.com recently to help me sell my domain names, and have found their service to be extremely useful. If you do have an active Estibot subscription, and you're paying $49.95 per month or higher, then you'll have access to the End-User Lead Generator.

This impressive tool allows you to enter any domain name into the system, and within minutes you'll be given a report containing possible leads for your domain name sales. Estibot uses data such as advertising profiles, domain keywords, meta keywords and page titles to present you with a list of sales leads.

Some of these leads may be unsuitable, so you'll need to go through each lead to see whether they're a suitable buyer. Out of 100 leads, I may only contact 15 or 20 of them.

Note: When using Estibot's Lead Generator, refrain from using the "Contact This Lead" function, as this will send an email to the site's WhoIs address, which as you'll know, in most circumstances isn't a good thing to do.

Once you've found all of your leads and have written each of them in your spreadsheet, you'll want to send your email to your end users.

Why You Should Concentrate on "End Users"

Before we move on to the sales email that you'll send, I wanted to tell you why you should be selling to end users instead of domainers.

An end user is a person or a company in the industry or profession that is related to your domain name. In most cases the right end user will pay a higher price for the domain name you own. This is because an end user will know the valuable data such as acquisition costs, how to compete in their industry and the value of an online presence to that company.

These factors will determine the end user's value of your domain name, and that value is normally far higher than a domainer will pay.

A domainer is a domain investor who is looking for a good price on a domain name to allow them to make the highest amount of money possible from that domain. A domain investor is far more likely to look at statistics such as sales history, CPC, number of searches per month and the amount of traffic the domain receives. A domain investor is also far more likely to offer a lower value for the domain name.

Whenever possible, you should always try to sell your domain names to end users to ensure that you get the maximum profit possible.

Your sales email

Once you've gathered all of the data for your end user and have placed that data into a spreadsheet, we're ready to start sending out emails to your prospective buyers. I'll be using Gmail, Boomerang and Sidekick (all mentioned previously) to show you how to send your emails.

The email address

Go to www.gmail.com in your Google Chrome browser (if you're using Boomerang and Sidekick) and create a new email. You'll be sending each email to one person at a time. This ensures that your emails are far more personal and you can include personalized facts and figures in each domain sales letter that you send.

Paste the first email address in your blank email, and move on to the subject field.

The Subject

The subject of your domain sales email is very important. If your email subject isn't interesting or attractive enough, there's a chance that your email will be deleted without being read. To give your email the highest chance of being opened, you need to use an enticing one-liner.

Here are two of the subject lines that I've tried and had poor success rates with:

- [DomainName] – purely listing the domain name in the subject field without any other words, giving the subject no context.
- Domain For Sale – this is too general and could be flagged up by spam filters.

The best subject line that I've used, and continue to use is: *[DomainName] is for sale*. This usually ensures that the email is opened by anyone who's interested in the domain name. It also gets past spam filters and lets the end user know exactly what's in the email.

The Message

We've come to the most important part: what do you say in your domain sales email message? I've sent thousands of domain sales emails in the last year or two and have noticed that some message templates get far more of a response than some others.

The points that I've taken away from my experiences of selling to end users are:

1. Keep the message fairly short. Say what you need to say without saying too much. A couple of paragraphs should be enough. Any longer than that and you're in danger of your recipient simply deleting the email.
2. Personalize the email. Don't simply copy & paste each email. Mention the recipient's name in the message and add any valuable statistics if necessary.
3. Include selling points to help convince the buyer that your domain is worth buying. If it's a valuable keyword domain name, let them know that the domain name can be resold for a profit.
4. Let the recipient know that you are contacting other similar companies (if you are). This will add a sense of urgency to the email without sounding desperate. It'll

let the recipient know that they need to act quickly if they want to own the domain name.

5. Always include your signature. Remember earlier when I recommended setting up a signature on your emails? Make sure to use that signature when contacting an end user. It provides the end user with a level of trust to see your email address and phone number listed.

I have thought about the pros and cons of including a sample email message here, and I've decided not to include a domain sales email template here. This is done to ensure that we don't all copy and paste the same email message to hundreds of buyers. If a particular end user receives the exact same message from two or more different sellers, then it may affect all of us.

So, for that reason I won't be including a domain sales email template. However, using the pointers above, you should be able to craft your own sales message. Over time you may wish to adapt it to try out new variations to see what works, and what doesn't.

How to make sure you don't end up in the spam folder

Our sales emails may sometimes be misconstrued for spam, and some strict filters will send our emails directly to the spam folder without even being read.

The only chance of staying out of the spam folder is to know why your emails may be seen as spam. According to a recent ReturnPath study, 10-20% of emails are lost to strict spam filters. There's no way to avoid a spam filter, so *we* need to avoid & include certain things:

1. **Avoid Spam Trigger Words:** Every spam filter has a series of trigger words. If it detects the use of these words, then chances are that you'll end up in the spam folder. There are hundreds of combinations of words which may alert the spam filter. Here are some of the most common trigger words:

    - Earn$
    - Clearance
    - Money making
    - Extra income
    - Additional income

- $$$
- Save $
- Investment
- Why pay more?
- Friend/Hello (Greeting)
- Click below
- Increase your sales
- Urgent

This list could cover at least five pages, but for the sake of my sanity I'm stopping it there. However, you'll get the idea of which words and phrases you should try not to include in your emails in order to stay out of the spam folder.

2. **Don't use a deceptive subject:** Any new emails which have deceptive subject lines, or start falsely with "RE:" or "FWD:" may be picked up by the spam filter. Keep your subject lines to

   "[DomainName] is for sale" or something similar.

3. **Don't bulk email:** if you send the same sales email to fifty people at the same time, an advanced spam filter may see this as a bulk spam message. Email your prospective buyers individually whenever possible.

4. **Use their names:** If you use the person's name and open your emails with "Hi [Name]" rather than simply "Hello" then you should be ok. It also improves that initial trust between the potential buyer and yourself.

5. **Include a signature:** Legitimate sales enquiries will use signatures, so you should do the same. Include your name, email address and phone number at the very least.

6. **Check your message first:** If you want to check whether your message is likely to be rejected by a spam filter, go to www.mail-tester.com to test out the message before you send it.

Should I Include A Price In My eMails?

I believe that you shouldn't include a price within your domain sales emails. If you decide to include a price within your email you may be excluding every single person that thinks your domain name is priced too high.

You'll no doubt be able to accept a lower offer than the price you list, but they don't necessarily know that and will more than likely simply pass on your offer due to the price you listed. You'll never know which recipients were interested in your domain name. At least if they reply with an offer you'll have the chance to negotiate with them.

If you include a price, a potential buyer may email back saying "No thank you, this domain is too expensive", which will end any sort of conversation. If you don't include a price, the same person may email you and say "How much is the domain?" - in which case, you know they're interested and can try to agree on a suitable price.

I'd recommend that instead of listing a price on your domain sales emails you should ask that the recipient replies with an offer if they're interested in acquiring the domain. From that point you can start to negotiate.

How many emails should I send?

If you've sent out your emails to the recipients and you don't receive any responses, or you don't receive any satisfactory offers, should you send out another email to all of those recipients? In my experience, this would be a bad thing to do.

If your recipients haven't replied to your first email, then I would take that as a sign that they're not interested in buying the domain name for whatever reason. By sending out more emails about your domain name you'll be potentially aggravating the recipient, giving yourself a bad reputation and giving the domain industry a bad reputation, too.

By sending multiple emails to your lists, you're also risking being added to blacklists or being reported to your ISP for spamming.

When should I send an email?

You can send an email to anyone at any time, but there is always an optimal time to send an email to a busy company owner or employee. I've found that you should avoid sending domain sales emails on:

- Monday – typically a busy day for employees who are looking to catch up with anything that's happened since Friday.
- Friday – a day when employees are looking to clear their desks and prepare for the weekend. On Friday

158

afternoons there may not be much work going on, and your email may not be read.

- Saturday – most business emails are not monitored over the weekend, meaning that your email will be on the bottom of a very big pile to look through on Monday.
- Sunday – the same as Saturday

I've found the highest read/response rate happens between Tuesday morning and Thursday lunchtime, and this is the period when I recommend sending your emails.

If you aren't able to send your emails at these times, then I'd recommend using
Boomerang to schedule your domain sales emails to send. Boomerang, as I said earlier in this book, is a Gmail service which allows you to send emails at specific times.

In terms of your domain sales letters, this means that you can write them when you have time – possibly one evening after work – and schedule them to be sent on Tuesday, Wednesday or Thursday.

Holidays

When sending out your sales emails, you'll need to be aware of national holidays in other countries. I'm based in the UK, but sell most of my domain names to American businesses. The USA and the UK share very few public holidays, so it's essential to be aware of any holidays. For example, sending sales letters in the week of Thanksgiving (last Thursday in November in the USA) should be avoided. Most staff will be trying to clear their desks in time for the Thanksgiving extended weekend, and it's highly likely your email will not be opened.

If you go to www.timeanddate.com/holidays you'll be able to see the holidays for various countries around the world. Doing business with countries other than
your own means that knowing their public holidays could be vital.

Monitoring Your Email Open Rates

Earlier on I introduced you to Sidekick – a free service which tracks your emails to see exactly when your emails have been opened. Use Sidekick to monitor which companies have opened your emails and how many times they've done so.

I'd also recommend adding this data to the spreadsheet which I mentioned earlier to allow you to accurately work out email open rates vs response rates.

Convincing A Buyer

How do you actually convince your recipient that your domain name is worth investing thousands of dollars in? Fortunately, you don't need to be a natural salesperson to sell a domain name if you did, I'd have sold precisely 0 domain names.

However, convincing a recipient to actually buy your domain name can be difficult. Some domain names sell themselves. You don't need to convince some buyers – they'll see the value in the domain name and will want to own it.

Some don't realize the value or potential of a domain name, and may think that you're simply trying to scam them. This is why including some convincing statements in your sales emails may be a good idea.

There are various statements you can include depending on the domain name you're selling:

1. You can sell the domain name on – let the end user know that the domain name is an asset rather than another online marketing cost. It can be sold on if it isn't needed.

2. The domain can offer instant credibility – if it's a truly premium domain name, then owning it can give instant credibility to the company, and can give consumers a level of instant trust.

3. Does the domain name have type in traffic already? If so, mention this. Type in traffic is easy to convert into sales for the right company.

4. It'll help with natural search rankings. Search engines attach more weight to premium exact match domains. I know that the power of exact match domains has dwindled somewhat in the past couple of years, but a well-developed website on an exact match domain name can improve natural search rankings. This means that the company may be able to spend less money on paid advertising for that search term.

What If No One Buys My Domain?

If you have sent out some emails and have received a few replies asking how much the domain name is, then you know that there are people out there who do have an interest in your domain. However, you may find that although you get some interest in your domain, you may not be able to close a sale. This may be because the price is too high.

On this occasion, I have started to use a technique that I read from Elliot Silver's DomainInvesting.com blog. He shared a tip which I've used to some effect, which is to email those who expressed interest for a second time with a lower Buy It Now (BIN) price for the domain.

If the price was too high, then emailing with a lower price may encourage your prospective buyer to acquire the name there and then. Here's how it's done.

Wait until around a week after you've sent your original domain sales email. Keep a record of everyone who's expressed interest in the domain name. If you haven't managed to close a sale, then send an email to everyone who was interested (email individually rather than sending a bulk email), saying that you've opted to drop the price of your domain name to ensure a fast sale.

State the domain name's new price, and let them know that you've sent the same email to other companies that were interested in your domain, and that the first to reply will get to own the domain name.

To ensure a sale, make sure that the price has been sufficiently cut to make it worth emailing again. For example, if you were selling a domain name for $550, consider dropping to a $350 Buy It Now price.

If you don't get any response from this email, then don't email for a third time. Leave the domain name unsold and perhaps try to re-open a negotiation nearer the domain's expiry date.

Contacting End Users Via Phone?

Should you ever contact end users via phone? I never have. I've always found that email has worked well for me. It's something that I'm comfortable with. I wouldn't be comfortable with selling over the phone, so I don't do that. I've also found that 9/10 buyers are comfortable with dealing with a domain name sale via email.

If you are comfortable with selling over the phone, then it may be something you're interested in trying. However, I believe that speaking to the right person via phone may be difficult – especially when you're dealing with a large company.

A main switchboard may not know where to direct your call, or if you're hoping to speak with a specific person, then you may not be able to get through to them. I've found that finding the right email address is a better way to make initial contact. If they want to carry on the negotiations via phone, then that's possible. At least then you'll be speaking directly to the decision maker.

Ensuring You Don't Spam

In 2003 the US Government introduced the CANSPAM act (Controlling the Assault of Non-Solicited Pornography and Marketing). This act has given us a list of rules that we must follow.

A little known fact about CAN-SPAM is that the act doesn't just apply to the sending of bulk emails. It covers all commercial messages, and could extend to domain sales emails if certain rules aren't followed.

Firstly, you should make sure that all of your domain sales emails are targeted. You should ensure that each recipient of your domain sales emails would have a genuine interest in owning the domain name because of the industry that they're in or the interest they have in the specific keyword(s) in your domain name. Simply emailing hundreds of people with similar domain names to yourself would be against the CANSPAM act.

Secondly, CAN-SPAM asks that you include a valid postal address with each email that you send out.

Thirdly, your subject line must accurately represent what is written within your emails. Misrepresentation of your content is against the CAN-SPAM rules.

There is also a rule about including an unsubscribe button, but from what I understand, a one-off email like ours should not need to include any type of unsubscribe button.

I'm not a lawyer, so it may be worth consulting someone with far more knowledge than myself, but as I see it you should be complying with the CAN-SPAM act if you follow the points above. For more information on the CAN-SPAM act, visit Google.

By the way – if you're caught breaking the CAN-SPAM rules, there is a fine of $16,000 for each email you send which breaks those rules.

Sales Multiples

If you are trying to work out an accurate sales price for your domain name, you may be interested in using sales multiples to maximize your profits from one domain name sale. Sales multiples are usually calculated in percentages.

Anything that's less than a 100% profit usually isn't worth your time. An example of a 100% profit would be buying a domain name for $69 and selling it for $138. After calculating the time taken to find sales leads and taking into account the fact that you'll need to give the government it's share, you'll find that buying a domain for $69 and selling for $138 won't be worth your time.

I try to sell a $69 domain name for at least $250, giving a 262% markup value. Of course, if your research shows that your domain may be worth far more, then charge accordingly. But as a rule, a good base line is around a 250% markup for your $69 domain names.

The largest domain sales markup I've ever had is 14,500%.

Lease To Own

I want to introduce you to the idea of lease to own sales. If your prospective buyer doesn't have the full budget to buy a domain name, but is still interested in acquiring the domain then you may wish to introduce a lease to own agreement.

A lease to own agreement allows you to complete a sale even if the domain name's price is out of your buyer's budget. The formation of a lease to own agreement for a domain name normally includes a percentage payment up front, followed by monthly payments.

For example, if you are negotiating for a lease to own agreement on a domain name that you've priced at $2,500 you could do the following:

1. A payment of $500 up front (20% of the purchase price)
2. 12 subsequent payments of $167 per month

During the lease to own agreement term, the buyer will be able to use the domain name as they see fit, but you'll still own the domain name. Once that final payment has been paid, you'll then transfer the domain name to the new owner.

Lease-to-own agreements can become more complicated than that – with many domain owners expecting balloon payments at the end of the term, or charging interest on monthly payments. Whatever you agree on, it should always be formally agreed upon in a legally binding contract, and it's also advisable to use an Escrow company to manage the monthly payments.

What To Do When A Recipient is a Complete *Asshole*

You may have already come across this problem already. If you haven't, be prepared to find this out for yourselves: there are a small number of people that you email who will reply to your emails with insults, derogatory comments or good old fashioned abuse.

This means that you'll have to have a level of callousness when sending out your sales emails. Expect to find an email in your inbox every so often that is telling you to F**k Off or generally insulting you for "being a domain squatter".

However tempting it is to reply to these people, just don't. It may be tempting to reply, but it's never good to do so from a professional point of view. Say, for example that you are selling a real estate domain name and you've sent out an email to ten local real estate agents.

If you receive one rude email, and reply to that with something sarcastic or rude, then there may be a chance that the recipient could email all other real estate agents in the area warning them that you're unprofessional, and send back nothing but abuse. That's your chance of a sale ruined.

It's just better to not give them any attention at all. Delete the email and make sure to never email them again.

Low-ballers

There is a term used in the domain industry frequently, which is a low-baller. These are individuals who see domain names as being worth $10 a piece, and don't understand the effectiveness of a premium domain name. You may receive plenty of these lowball offers.

Recently I received a lowball offer via the DomainNameSales.com platform. It was a domain name which I'd expect to sell for around $2,500. I received a $10 offer stating that if I wasn't going to use the domain name, they'd pay me the registration fee so that they could use it.

If and when you get lowball offers on premium domain names that you genuinely think are worth hundreds or thousands of dollars, then simply send a counter offer with your asking price. Perhaps they're a person that won't pay more than $10 for your domain name. On the other hand, the offer may be their way of opening negotiations. It's not a good tactic, but I believe that you should never just ignore an offer: there's someone who's willing to buy your domain name, and there's a chance that you may be able to negotiate them up to closer to your original asking price.

It's not something that happens often, but I have heard stories of a $10 opening offer ending in a four figure sale.

Using A Domain Broker

If you aren't aware of what a domain broker is or does, then I'll briefly explain. A domain broker is someone who can help to negotiate with a company or an individual on your behalf. They're usually experienced with selling domain names to large companies for large sums of money.

Domain buyers use brokers, too. Companies such as Microsoft, Coca Cola and Google regularly use brokers to obscure the identity of the buyer. This is usually to ensure that they don't over pay for a domain name that they need. (Imagine finding out that Microsoft needs a domain name that you own. You'd add an extra 0 onto the price, wouldn't you?)

Is it ever justified to use a domain broker to sell your domain names? Yes, of course.

Domain brokers usually know who to contact within a company and how to contact them. Top domain name brokers such as Andrew Rosener of MediaOptions.com routinely sell to large companies. Brokers may also have lists of contacts/buyers who are always interested in certain types of domain names.

I personally like to negotiate my own deals, and haven't used a domain broker to sell any of my domain names. I'm not the best negotiator by far, but I enjoy learning the art of negotiation and I believe it's a skill that can be transferred to the wider world.

I believe that if you are in a position where you're trying to close a deal with a larger company and are having difficulty getting to the right people, or you're having problems closing the deal – possibly because one department is refusing to sign off on the deal, then a domain broker will be able to act on your behalf to use their expertise to help close the deal quickly.

Whenever you use a domain name broker, be prepared to pay a 10-20% commission. A fair price to pay for a good domain broker.

Negotiating Your Domain Sale

As I mentioned previously, I'm not the best negotiator in the world and I'm constantly learning, but I do feel that I've learned enough from some of the best in the business to be able to pass on some knowledge to you.

There are two examples of domain negotiations I'm going to take you through: enquiries that have come from your domain sales emails and enquiries that have come via a parked page or WhoIs details.

It can be difficult to know how much the domain name is worth and how much the prospective buyer is willing to spend. These are things that you must work out based on statistics and recent sales. The most important thing to do is to know how much you want for the domain name. Don't be over-realistic (for example, don't expect $100,000 for a $500 domain name) as buyers will usually have a good idea of how much a domain is worth to them, and they won't pay much more than that.

If your prospective buyer can't match or come close to your expected price, then don't be afraid to end negotiations. You also need to know when you receive a good offer for a domain name. If you're unsure of a domain name's value in the face of an offer that you've received, then don't be afraid to ask for opinions from other domainers. Posting an appraisal request on NamePros or DNForum.com can be useful.

Firstly, let's look at enquiries that have come via your domain sales emails. You've sent out an email to your prospective buyers, and the buyer has replied. There are two things that could happen here:

1. They make an initial offer for your domain name
2. The reply simply asking "How Much?"

Here's how I deal with both types of enquiries.

For the first type of response in which your prospective buyer makes an initial offer for your domain name, you've got to understand that you have lost some ground already. When offering your domain name for sale, you're likely to receive a lower price because you're actively selling. If you're not actively selling, but your prospective buyer is desperate to buy your domain, then you'd be in total control, and could ask a higher price.

With that in mind, you should analyze their initial offer. Is it a fee that is close to your own appraisal of the domain name? Is it too low to consider selling? Do you think you could ask for more money from the buyer?

This all depends on your own situation. If you are desperately needing a sale, then the circumstances may mean that you accept their initial offer for fear that a deal may not be reached if you reject their first offer. However, if you believe the domain name is worth more, then test the waters and tell them the price you had in mind. When stating a firm price in this situation, be prepared for some bargaining. The buyer may improve their offer, but may not be willing to meet your full price.

Depending on who your buyer is and how keen they are to buy the domain name, these negotiations could take hours, days, weeks or months. I've found that in almost all cases, the initial offer is not the final price that they're willing to pay. I've had $500 offers quickly turn into $2,500 sales because I said that their original offer was too low.

You may wish to reply with a counter offer. They'll either accept the counter offer, reject the counter offer or send an improved offer.

The second response in which the prospective buyer is asking for a price needs to be handled slightly differently. When pricing your domain names in this situation you need to take into account who the buyer is, how much you paid for the domain name, how they can use the domain name (think about CPC and customer acquisition costs) and recent similar sales. These factors along with your own appraisal of the domain name will give you a price.

The reply needs to be straight to the point – stating your price and little else. For example:

Hi [Name],

I would accept a price of $[Price] for the domain name.

From there it's their decision. They'll weigh up whether the domain name is worth that price to them. They might even reply with a lower offer. In which case you can either accept the offer or negotiate higher. It's up to you, and it all depends on how much of a risk you want to take.

The time between your reply and their response is important. Don't email the prospective buyer again until you've heard from them. This could be days or weeks, but leave it to them. During a negotiation like this you may leave money on the table if you come across as desperately wanting to close the deal.

There are very few things that the movie The Wolf Of Wall Street taught me. However, there was one line that Leonardo DiCaprio used that I have always remembered. He was teaching his employees how to sell over the phone, and he said: "Whoever speaks first loses". I believe that to be true in this situation. If you speak first, you'll leave money on the table.

The second example that I'm going to take you through is when a buyer contacts you. This could be done either through a parking platform (such as DomainNameSales.com), or via email through the WhoIs contact details – incidentally, make sure that your WhoIs details are always up to date.

In this scenario, you are on top. Your prospective buyer has researched the domain name and possibly taken steps to find out how much the domain name is worth. You've got to also remember that your domain name is unique, so if they want your domain name, they'll have to negotiate with you and they'll have to agree a price with you.

In order to close a deal, you'll need to know how to reply to the offers that you receive.

A typical message you'll be sent to enquire about your domain name is:

Hi,

I am interested in [domainname].com. Is it for sale? If so, what's the price?

Regards,

[Buyer's Name]

There are two questions that may immediately come to mind:

1. How do I reply to this email?
2. When should I reply to this email?

There are two schools of thought on how to reply to a request like this. Some say that asking the buyer to make an offer is the best thing to do. This enables you to see how much the buyer is willing to spend, and enables you to see whether the buyer really is serious.

I'm of the opinion that stating a firm price to start with is the best thing to do. You state your price, and if the prospective buyer can't match it, then that's their problem. When you receive an enquiry, the most important thing to know is that you should be in total control of those negotiations. As I mentioned above, you have the upper hand because you own a unique domain name. At the same time, you also want to bear in mind that some companies have different options for domain names – if the price you're quoting is too high, they may simply walk away and buy a different domain name.

The first thing that I always like to do when I receive a new enquiry is to try and find out who is sending you the offer. If you don't know who you're dealing with, then you'd better find out quickly. Usually by doing a Google search for their name and email address you can find some valuable data that may help with your negotiations. For example, your research may find that your buyer might be acting on behalf of a large company. In which case you know that they may well have a healthy budget for your domain name.

If you receive a sales enquiry through the DomainNameSales.com platform, much of the work is done for you. You'll be able to see their name, email address, phone number and their location. Using this can tell you more about any prospective buyer. It's a step that I always take before replying to any offer.

Once you've established who they are, send them your firm (but reasonable) price. It's then up to them to come back with any offer, or to accept your price. Adding an offer expiry time may be useful, too. For example after stating your price, tell the prospective buyer that the price is only valid for 7 days.

As for when you should send your reply, I believe that replying within an hour or two of receiving the enquiry is right. Replying straight away may come across as too keen, but delaying your response for days or weeks may mean the person/company has moved on to another domain name.

If the prospective buyer comes back with an offer – or if they open with an offer – you should know that this usually won't be their maximum offer. No one starts with their highest offer. Which is why you should try to counter with a higher offer. They may accept this offer, or they may improve their original offer.

If you can't agree a price, let the negotiations end on an open note, letting them know that if they can match your asking price then they can renegotiate in the future. If a price can be agreed upon then it's time to start working out all aspects of the domain name transaction.

Using Escrow.com should be a part of all of your end user domain name sales. Many buyers will not have heard of Escrow.com so it's your job to introduce this topic. Escrow.com also requires a fee to be paid to use their service, and there are three options as to who pays that fee:

1. Buyer pays the fee
2. Seller pays the fee
3. The fee is split between buyer and seller

Options one and three are most commonly used.

You should also consider where the domain name needs to be transferred to. Some buyers will insist on transferring the domain name to their own registrar and account and others will be happy to simply use the registrar in which the domain name is currently hosted. This is something you'll need to know before finalizing your deal.

When you do need to either transfer your domain or initiate an account change, your current registrar should be able to help you if you are unsure of any of the procedures.

Domain Sales Example

For the purpose of this book, I decided to show you an example of the strategy that is
played out here. The domain in question is
BleepTest.com. I found it using ExpiredDomains.net, and bought it via SnapNames for $69.

I left the domain name for a week, parked at DomainNameSales.com. I could see it got some traffic, but had no revenue. I then decided to sell it and look through Google for other companies and websites using the term Bleep Test (or a similar term Beep Test).

I found five suitable candidates to sell the domain name to, and sent each of them a sales letter. The subject of my email was "BleepTest.com Domain For Sale", and I crafted individual sales emails based on how I thought the domain name could help their business.

I used Sidekick to monitor the open rates, and sent out my emails on a Thursday morning. By Thursday night, I had three separate offers for the domain name, and eventually negotiated a sale with the highest offer of $230.

The domain name transaction took place through PayPal, with 50% of the fee being paid before the domain name was transferred. The remaining 50% was then paid. This type of sale (50% before, 50% after) is always done at your own risk.

This domain sale certainly isn't a record breaker, but it shows that this system does work – it allowed me to get a $161 profit within two weeks by just sending out five sales emails.

Chapter 8: Selling Domains At The Marketplaces

Domain name marketplaces are excellent for safely connecting with end users who are looking for new domain names – perhaps for an existing website or for a new project. With hundreds of domain names sold every week across the major domain marketplaces, it's vital to list your domain names with these marketplaces in order to give your domain name's the maximum exposure possible.

How To Sell Domains At Sedo.com

Sedo.com is one of the largest domain name marketplaces in existence, and routinely sells over a million dollars' worth of domain names a week. Sedo attracts a large amount of end users who trust the brand to obtain domain names safely and easily.

For this reason, listing your domain names at Sedo should be a must. To do this, you'll first need to create an account at Sedo.com. Once you've done this, go to My Account and click on Add Domains. Here, you'll be able to add all the domain names that you need to.

Sedo will then verify your ownership of the domain names (usually a process which is complete within a day), and then your domain names will be live on the website and available for prospective buyers to see.

However, you'll want to modify your domain names to edit their categories and prices. Some people search for specific domain names on Sedo, but the majority seem to browse through categories to find suitable domains, so you'll need to ensure that your categories are correct. To do this, you'll need to go back into your Sedo account and click on Manage Domains. You'll be presented with a table of your domain names along with valuable information such as the domain's category, minimum offer value and domain's price.

Firstly, try to ensure that your domain names are listed in the correct categories – many Sedo users may browse through relevant categories to find the right domain name for them, so use the category system to your advantage – if you have a specific niche domain name, make sure that you choose the right category.

After you've done that, check the minimum offer of your domain names. The minimum offer section ensures that if any offers made on your domain names must be over a certain value. If a user tries to submit a low bid for your domain, Sedo will automatically notify them that the offer is too low.

Another advantage of the minimum offer system is that you know that if someone does submit an offer and can meet your minimum offer value, you're dealing with a serious buyer and can negotiate your position accordingly.

I always put a minimum $200 offer on my domain names as I know that anyone who can match or surpass this amount is likely to be able to spend a lot more on the domain name.

The third and final option for managing your domain names in Sedo is the Buy It Now option. If this is activated, it will give Sedo user's the option to buy the domain name straight away for a set value. I haven't experimented too much with this Buy

It Now option, and have personally preferred to set my domain names to "Make An Offer" rather than Buy It Now as I prefer to negotiate with my potential buyers to ensure I don't leave money on the table.

I do, however think I understand the psychology behind using Sedo's Buy It Now system.

In fact, Sedo are encouraging domain owners to set domain names as Buy It Now. Recently, as much as 51% of domain name sales have been via Buy It Now.

Sedo's philosophy is that Buy It Now domain names tend to sell faster than Make An Offer domain listings. You can see why this may be the case. Imagine that you're an end user with no experience of domain names, but you know that securing the right name may cost a couple of thousand dollars. You see the domain name that you want to buy, but it's a Make Offer listing. You're daunted by the prospect of entering into a negotiation. On the other hand, if that same buyer is given a Buy It Now price, they can decide relatively quickly if they can match that price, and can then buy the domain name there and then without having to deal directly with the seller.

Whatever you decide to do, you need to remember that Sedo charges a 15% commission with a minimum $50 charge, so you'll need to price your domain names with that in mind.

How To Sell Domains At GoDaddy.com

GoDaddy – the world's largest registrar. And seemingly the world's largest commission rate, too: a 30% commission on domain names you sell through their premium listings website. They do have a large user base though, so it's worth listing your domains here. Just remember that any price here has to take into consideration that commission rate.

If your domain names are registered with GoDaddy, you can advertise your names for free using Premium Listings. For a 30% commission, your domain names are shown in user domain name searches. Have you ever tried to register a domain at GoDaddy and seen a notification saying that the domain name is available to register for thousands of dollars for the first year? That's a premium listing. If a buyer wants your domain name, all they have to do is add it to the cart, pay your price and the domain will be transferred to them.

To add your domains to Premium Listings, go to your GoDaddy Domain Manager, select the domain names that you want to add to Premium Listings, click on the Monetize button and select Sell on Premium Listing.

From there you'll be taken through the stages to list your domain names. After they've been activated, your domains will appear in relevant user searches – giving your domain names a fair amount of exposure to potential end users.

Premium Listing domain names must be registered with GoDaddy. For other means of selling at GoDaddy.com, you could sell through their auction website. To do this, you first need to sign up to a GoDaddy Auction account at a cost of $4.99 per year.
Then, go to http://auctions.godaddy.com and go to Selling List → List A Domain. From there you can create your listings.

GoDaddy is the world's largest domain registrar and actively advertises to a general audience. You'll have no doubt seen their adverts during the Super Bowl, and they also advertise during the English Premier League. A wide user base means more potential buyers for your domains, so if your domain name is registered at GoDaddy, take advantage of their Premium Listing service.

How To Sell Domains At DomainNameSales.com

DomainNameSales.com has been mentioned a few times within this book, chiefly because I believe that DNS are the best parking and sales management platform that you can use. It's a complex system that was developed by Frank Schilling to initially manage the parking and sales of his own large portfolio of domains. He's since opened it up to other domain investors.

As well as offering domain parking services, you can access the state-of-the-art sales portal, designed to help manage your domain inquiries and to help you effectively sell your domains. The typical domain transaction on DomainNameSales.com starts with an enquiry or offer via the parking page.

Assuming you've added your domain names to their system and your domains are now parked with DomainNameSales.com, you will now be able to start receiving offers on your domain names. Prospective buyers will be able to enquire about a domain name you own via the DomainNameSales.com marketplace, or by a for sale link from your domain's parked page.

Once the prospective buyer has made contact, you'll be notified via email (or by the DomainNameSales.com app, if you have it) that you have a new enquiry. You'll be able to see all of the details of that enquiry from the DomainNameSales.com sales management system. The details you get here include the buyer's name, email address, phone number and location. All very useful when you're trying to find out exactly who your buyer is.

I love the sales platform at DomainNameSales.com, it's so easy to manage your leads. You can reply to your leads using email templates, you can craft your own email responses, you can set reminders to be sent to the prospective buyer periodically.

The DomainNameSales.com system is free to use. However, you do have an option to send your leads to the DomainNameSales.com brokerage team. It's their job to get you the best price possible – they talk to the buyer via email or phone and negotiate on your behalf. In return for this, you'll be charged at 10% commission on your domain sales.

A fee which is worth paying to have some of the world's best domain name brokers working for you.

As with Sedo and GoDaddy, you have the option to include a Buy It Now price, which can be activated through your domain management panel.

How To Sell Domains At Afternic.com

I want to start off by saying that I've never sold a domain name through Afternic.com, although I regularly read of high sales figures, so they do have a very active sales base.

To make sure that as many people see your domains as possible via Afternic, you'll want to list your domain names with their premium service. The Afternic premium service exposes your domain names to around 80 million searches per month, thanks to partnerships with 18 of the 25 top registrars in the world.

In return for this exposure, you'll pay a 20% commission rate to Afternic.com. As always, adjust your pricing to incorporate this commission.

Afternic is now owned by GoDaddy, but it seems to be running independently for now.

The marketplaces listed above are just a part of a good domain sales strategy, and all involve getting your domain names listed at as many places as possible to ensure maximum exposure for your domains.

Chapter 9: Portfolio Management

An important part of a successful domaining strategy is to manage your portfolio of domain names. This means using spreadsheets to keep a track of sales, offers, expiry dates, parking revenue and other important data. If you do this now when you have relatively few domain names, then it'll become second nature if you start to increase the number of domain names in your portfolio.

Create A Spreadsheet

Yes, it's another spreadsheet! I loathe spreadsheets and keeping a track of data, but I've found that it's the only way to keep track of everything to do with my domain names. This could be quite time consuming to start with, but doing this regularly will really help with most aspects of your domain name management.

Column 1: The domain names.

First of all, you'll need to input every domain name that you own. Include all of your personal domain names, too. Doing this ensures that you have a record of all of your domain names and can refer to them whenever you need to.

Column 2: Expiry Date.

Include the expiry date of every domain name so that you are aware of every renewal fee that you'll need to pay. The week preceding the expiry date would be a good time to decide whether or not you want to renew the domain name. It's also a good time to look for current discount codes to get money off your renewal fees.

Column 3: Registrar

Make a note of your domain name registrar. I have domain names dotted around in several accounts at several registrars, so knowing where each domain name is registered is helpful. Especially when you start to build your portfolio.

Column 4: Your Plans

What are your plans for the domain name? You have many options here: do you want to drop the domain, actively sell the domain, develop the name or hold onto the name? You should review this regularly as your plans and circumstances change.

Column 5: Sales Price

Has the domain name already sold? If so, post your sales price here. Keeping track of your past sales is very helpful, especially when it comes around to taxes.

Column 6: Parking Revenue

If your domain names are parked, then post your latest parking revenue figures here.

Decide upon a constant time frame: for example, parking revenue for the past 3 months. Figures such as these will help to decide whether or not to renew the domain name.

Column 7: Offers received

Have you received any offers for the domain name? Write these down a numerical value every time you receive an offer, no matter what the offer is – even if it's a $10 offer. It shows that someone is interested in buying your domain name.

Column 8: Nameservers

Where do your domain names point? Are they parked, are they used to host a website? Write down details about the nameservers in column 8 to keep track of what your domain names are doing. There have been plenty of times where I've forgotten to change nameservers of new domain names that I own. If any of your domain names still point to default registrar pages instead of a parked page or a website, then you may be losing out on offers or parking revenue.

Every time you buy a new domain name, add it to the list and review the information for the other domain names. Make sure it's all up to date. As I said earlier, doing this every time you buy or register a new domain name can help to keep track of things as your portfolio increases in size.

Auto Renew?

There's a feature used by almost all domain name registrars called auto renew. It's a feature that allows you to renew your domain names automatically without you having to log in and pay manually.

But is it a feature that you should be using? By default (with many registrars) the auto renew feature is switched on, meaning that in a year the registrar will deduct the renewal fees from your credit card and extend the registration for another year.

It can be such a useful feature with some of your domain names, but should you use it on all of your domain names? No. As I said, it's a great feature for some of your domain names. Those names that I'd recommend turning auto renew on for are:

- Personal domain names – your own name or your family names
- Development domains – if you have any websites that you're developing then renewing the registration period automatically can be helpful.
- Your most valuable domain names – do you have any domains that bring in a lot of parking revenue, or do you receive a lot of offers on any domain names? Renew them automatically to avoid losing the names.

For the rest of your domain names, I'd advise reviewing your domain before renewing manually. For example – is there a domain name that you bought in the hope of flipping that hasn't given you the success you thought? Have you had no offers or traffic on the domain name? Then you may look to drop that domain name when the renewal period comes around.

Your registrar will usually send you plenty of reminder emails to let you know that your domain is expiring, so you'll need to make your decision after seeing one of these emails. If you plan to let the domain drop, then ignore any subsequent emails prompting you to renew the domain name.

Monitor Discount Codes

Everyone loves a discount code. At many times during the year, the major registrars will release various discount codes designed to attract new customers and to retain old ones. GoDaddy, for example, releases hundreds of discount codes every year.

Regularly checking websites such as http://livecodes.blogspot.com (if your domains are registered with GoDaddy) will give you the opportunity to save some money on domain name renewals or new registrations.

Renewal discount codes do exist, but they're harder to find. So, if you do find a renewal code that gives you a substantial discount then renew as many domain names as you can (that you were planning to renew anyway).

Whilst I'm writing about discounts and GoDaddy, I want to mention GoDaddy's Domain Discount Club which may be of interest if you have a large portfolio of domain names. Essentially, the Domain Discount Club is a subscription-based club which gives you access to exclusive GoDaddy discounts. It currently costs $9.99/month for a 12 month subscription and in return you can currently get a 45% discount on .com domain names. Other TLDs have between a 17% and 60% discount. It also includes a free GoDaddy Domain Auctions membership.

This is designed for members who register and renew domain names regularly – those with large portfolios (50+ domains) in other words.

What To Drop & What Not To Drop

Holding onto the wrong domain names can be a costly problem. Paying renewal fees every year for a domain name that has no chance of selling is a pretty pointless thing to do, and knowing when to drop your domain names is a valuable way of keeping your domain portfolio strong.

We'll start with what not to drop. These are my own recommendations based upon what I do with my own portfolio. Some of this advice has been given to me by others, and it's worked well for me so I'm passing it on to you:

- **Personal domain names:** Keep all of your personal domain names: family names, friend's names, your surname. Any domain names of that sort should be kept. These names can come in use for personal email addresses, personal websites, blogs and resumes.
- **Any domain producing revenue:** If any of your domain names are producing enough revenue every year to

cover their renewal fees (for .COM domains that's around $10), then keep them. If these domain names are paying for themselves, then you can afford to wait until the right offer comes along.

- **Any domain name that's had an offer to buy:** Remember earlier when I recommended listing every offer you've received on your domain name?
  This is why. It makes this section slightly easier. Domain names that have had offers on them should be kept. Even if those offers are low, it shows that someone is interested in the domain name, and more than likely the right buyer will come along eventually.
- **Development domain names:** Any name that you've earmarked for development should be kept for as long as you are serious about the project.

You could either set these domain names to autorenew or review these names every time they come up for renewal. Although these are all recommendations, you should always pay close attention to your financial situation and never let your renewal fees take money that should be used elsewhere.

As for domain names that should be dropped, here they are:

- **Anything that doesn't make sense:** If you have any domain names that you've already registered that don't particularly make sense, or are questionable in any way, allow these domain names to expire.

- **Trademarks:** review your domain name keywords with a site such as USPTO.gov to see whether any of your domains contain trademarked terms. If they do, delete the domain names now. Otherwise there is a possibility that the trademark owners will come after you.

- **Domains with no revenue, traffic or offers:** If any domain name hasn't produced revenue *and* they haven't received any purchase offers, then drop them. The chances are that no one will be interested in the domain name, and continued renewal will mean money is wasted.

- **Non .COM names:** Unless you own *ultra premium* keywords in other TLDs (such as .net or .info), then drop the names or look to sell them as soon as possible. Stick to .COM investments for now.

Don't Get Attached

There are many reasons why you may want to buy a domain name, and plenty more reasons as to why you may want to keep it. One of those reasons may be affection. I know, affection for a virtual string of numbers or letters may sound strange, but it does happen.

You may feel attached to a domain name because of the circumstances around your purchase, or maybe because it was one of your first domain purchases. I remember a certain domain name that I renewed year after year because it was one of the first domains I ever bought: PhotoshopClinic.com (yes, it's a trademark infringing name).

If you do get emotionally attached to any of your domain names, then you won't think logically. You'll bypass the steps mentioned above and simply renew the domain name year after year, with no hope of anyone buying the domain from you. Worse still is if you turn down an offer because you're so attached to the name!

Use statistics and logic over emotion to make decisions about your domain names, otherwise you could be wasting money on renewal fees year after year.

Managing Offers

If your domain names are good enough, you'll receive some offers from interested parties. Aside from negotiating with them (which I covered earlier), you'll want to know how to manage those offers.

I'd recommend keeping track of every offer which is sent to you. This is done so that you can monitor the popularity of your domain names, and it's also useful if you want to actively sell your domains in the future.

If you park your domain names with DomainNameSales.com, your inquiries can be archived in order to let you access them at a later point. If your domain names are parked with DomainNameSales.com, then use their system to archive leads. If none of those inquiries lead to a sale, that doesn't matter. Archive them anyway to ensure that you have leads when you come to actively sell the domain names.

DomainNameSales.com also lets you message older leads, which is a very useful feature.

Not as useful as the Old Lead Management system. Via this setting, you can allow DomainNameSales.com's brokers to contact unsuccessful leads to see whether a deal can be agreed to buy a domain you own.

For offers and enquiries which have been sent to your email address, use yet another spreadsheet to write these offers down in. Include the domain in question, their name, email address and offer price if they've placed an offer (rather than just an enquiry).

This ensures that you have all the relevant data should you ever need to contact them again, for example if you need to sell a domain name quickly, then sending out a sales email to those who you know were interested in the domain could give you a quick sale.

Portfolio Management Software

If you want a more substantial way of managing your domain names rather than a simple spreadsheet, then you may be interested in Watch My Domains software (www.watchmy.domains). This premium piece of software for both Mac and Windows allows you manage your portfolio effectively.

After inputting your list of domain names (which can be broken up into categories such as Personal and Business domains), the software will process the domain names and produce a spreadsheet with most of the valuable information that I mentioned above.

It lists the current expiry date, allows you to view the domain's Whois data, shows you the current nameservers, the domain creation date, domain status and more. This type of software can be useful when you start to build a larger portfolio of domain names.

It even shows a warning for domain names that are about to expire or have expired, which may alert you to that fact, prompting you to renew the domains. If you're looking for more than just a spreadsheet, then I recommend that you take a look at this piece of software.

It's currently a $49 program, and has been created by some very reliable developers who have created other programs that I've used in the past. This is the only piece of portfolio management software that I can recommend (apart from a basic spreadsheet, of course).

What To Do With Names You Plan To Drop

If you've chosen to let certain domain names expire rather than paying for renewal fees, you may be wondering what you should do with those domain names *before* they expire? Should you just leave them to expire, or should you try to sell them to cash in on your investment?

The chances are that you've decided to drop the domain name because it doesn't fit certain criteria such as the amount of revenue it makes or the amount of offers you've received for the domain name. In this case, it doesn't bode well in trying to sell the domain before it expires.

However, it's worth just five minutes of your time in trying to sell the domain name to someone for a cut price. At least you'll receive some cash for a domain that was going to be dropped anyway. I'd recommend posting some names on DNForum.com and

NamePros.com under their fixed price sections. Setting a fairly low (under $100) fixed price for your domains may attract some attention and may find you a buyer. I've done this successfully on a couple of occasions.

Your other alternative is to make sure that the dropping domains are listed on all the major marketplaces –

GoDaddy, Afternic, Sedo, DomainNameSales.com etc. Set a Buy It Now price and leave it. If you're lucky, someone may decide to match that Buy It Now price – in which case you've got extra money from a domain name that you were going to drop!

The reason why I've suggested using Buy It Now prices is that you don't want to invest much time at all in domain names that you're going to drop. Set a Buy It Now price and leave it. If someone buys, then it's good news! If no one buys, then stick to your original plan and let the domain expire.

Prepare Your Family To Take Over

If – God forbid – something were to happen to you, then your domain names and websites may be impossible for your family/friends to access. Your thousands of dollars worth of assets may simply expire.

You should put in place some procedures to help your family and friends with your assets if something does happen. I know this is a morbid subject, but it's better to act now and know that there are processes in place to make sure that your loved ones can benefit from your online assets.

This can be complicated as you'll have to make sure that someone knows to pay the yearly fees, manage parking accounts and respond to offers.

In years to come there will be legislation that is introduced to ensure that your digital assets can be handed over to a family member or a friend on your death, but for now we have to make other arrangements.

The user agreement on many online services is between the user and the service provider exclusively, which means that members of your family may not be able to access those accounts after your death unless you leave a document containing your usernames & passwords.

You may wish to use an estate planner to store all of this valuable information, or you could keep it in a sealed envelope with specific instructions to open this on your death.

I'd recommend including the following information within that document:

- A list of usernames and passwords for your domain registrar accounts, your email accounts, parking accounts and your hosting accounts. Obviously update this information if your passwords change.
- Contact details for those domain registrars and hosting companies, just in case your family members need to contact them. Include the current values of your domain names for

reference. If an offer is received on one of your domain names then your family/friends can use this value to gauge whether or not it's worth cashing the domain in.

- Contact details for friends within the domain industry. If you have trusted friends who are domainers, then include their contact details. They may be able to help your family to sell or maintain your domain investments. Many people will not have any idea as to how much domain names can be worth, so having knowledgeable contacts who can help your family is a good idea.

I felt that including this small section was justified and could stretch to other aspects of your digital life that may need planning for. For example – PayPal accounts, online bank accounts, eBilling systems and alike. As more of our lives move online, we need online asset protection if anything happens.

Chapter 10: Making Money From Development of Domains

Owning a domain portfolio is one thing, but how do you make money from them? We've covered domain sales in some depth in this book, but there are plenty of potentially lucrative alternatives to selling your domain names. I'll be going through each moneymaking solution in detail, and explaining exactly how you go about doing it.

Parking

Parking a domain name is essentially allowing adverts to be placed on your domain name in return for a cut of the advertising revenue. In the good old days of domaining, you could set your domain names to park and live off the advertising revenue. If you had a strong .COM portfolio you could make thousands of dollars a month without having to do anything.

There are still a minority of domain names that can do this. Rick Schwartz has been quoted as saying that Porno.com (currently parked at DomainNameSales.com) has made him around $10,000,000 since he acquired it in 1997 for $42,000.

The average revenue from domain parking has dropped over the years and has put many domain parking companies out of business. DomainNameSales.com has emerged as one of the leaders in domain parking thanks to its simple system and decent CPC rates.

If, like me, you own a decent portfolio of domain names with no outstanding ultrapremium .COM domains, then parking may not be the long term answer to creating a constant revenue stream. Of course, creating full websites on every domain name you own isn't viable and will be very time consuming, so a percentage of your domain names will probably be parked. As long as they make their renewal fees in revenue every year, they're OK being parked.

Waiting...

There are some domain investors that simply wait for offers to come in on their domain names, thus being in an excellent position to get the most money from a domain sale. These investors typically own hundreds or thousands of ultra-premium domain names and supplement their income with other websites, domain parking and day jobs.

I wouldn't advise trying to build a portfolio just to sit on and do nothing if like most of us you have bills that need to be paid each month.

Websites

Developing websites must now be the most popular way of monetizing your domain names. Website development is so accessible now that anyone can release a website within a matter of minutes. These websites can come in different types and complexities. Some may even be so successful that they can be run as a business on their own. There are many different website strategies that may work for you depending on what type of domain names you own.

WordPress

Before I start showing you each type of website that you might want to develop on your domain names, I'd like to introduce you to WordPress. For those that don't know,
WordPress runs around 25% of all websites on the Internet. It's such a versatile and simple platform to use that anyone can build a WordPress site and install themes and plugins.

To install WordPress, you need a hosting plan. At my own hosting plan with
SiteGround.com, I have the ability to install WordPress on a domain name by just filling out a couple of different options – their software does the rest for me. Most hosting accounts will have placed an "Install WordPress" button on your cPanel homepage, which is fairly easy to locate.

If you don't have that option, then manual installation isn't too difficult. WordPress have released a guide to installing WordPress which can be read here: http://codex.wordpress.org/Installing_WordPress

WordPress Plugins & Themes

The great thing about WordPress is that so many designers and developers create free and premium solutions to help us build the best websites possible. Plugins are additional pieces of software which can be installed on your WordPress system to give your website improved functionality. One popular example is Yoast – a free SEO (search engine optimization) plugin which helps to improve your on-site SEO.

The same can be said for themes. There are thousands of free and premium WordPress themes available online, and marketplaces such as ThemeForest.net have been very successful in selling premium WordPress themes. There is probably a theme out there for any type of WordPress project you could imagine – and they're all available for fairly reasonable prices, cutting down on any design and development costs.

WordPress Posts & Pages

WordPress websites are built on a system of posts and pages, with no limits on the amount of posts and pages you can create. If you have installed the WordPress system already, take a minute to have a look around your WP Admin panel to

225

familiarize yourself with the setup. Each example that I give below will be shown using a WordPress installation. You don't need coding or development experience to do this – it can all be done by you, without having to hire someone else.

Lead Generation

If you're unfamiliar with the term lead generation, it's a strategy used to create more business. This is done both online and offline and can be done by companies and individuals alike. Domain owners can easily profit from online lead generation by developing out their domain names and create a highly optimized website which is designed specifically for creating leads.

To do this, choose one of your domain names. I'd recommend starting with a local domain name if you have any. These are the simplest to create and market. For this example, I'm going to use a domain name that I own: ConnecticutElectrician.com. I caught the domain name as it dropped, and eventually paid around $18 for it. I think it's a fantastic name that could be sold on for a profit at some point, but for now I want to use the domain name to create a lead generation website for electricians across Connecticut.

My method of creating a lead generation website is to create the website first before attempting to create any partnerships with local companies, so we'll start by creating the website.

First of all, make sure that WordPress has been installed on your hosting plan, and your domain name is pointed to the correct nameservers. If you need help with this, your hosting company will be happy to help.

Once that's done, we'll want to choose the best theme in order to create a good local website. You have plenty of options when it comes to WordPress themes. However, there are just two themes which I've found work well; Blackriders by InkThemes and Genesis (Crystal child theme) by StudioPress.

These are both themes which work well because of their simplicity and versatility. They also currently include licenses which allow you to use the themes across a number of different websites, so once you've created your first website you'll be able to replicate your website & theme across a number of different domain names.

For this website, I'm going to buy the Blackriders theme at InkThemes.com. It's current'y $59 and has a number of features suited to building lead generation websites. I am using it for all of my domain name development projects at the moment.

You may be well aware of how to set up a WordPress theme by now, but for those that aren't, you need to log into your WordPress Admin panel and go to:

Appearance → Themes → Add New → Upload Theme.

Upload your theme, then go to Theme Options to add your logo, lead capture settings, slider settings and homepage feature areas.

Your logo doesn't have to be anything special, but if you can't create your own logo, there are cheap logo creation services available on oDesk, Fiverr or Freelancer.com. As for creating content to appear on the front page, you'll need to use your keywords, and their variants. My keywords are "Connecticut Electrician", so I'll be using those keywords as well as variants such as "Electricians in Connecticut", "Connecticut Electrical Services" and "Connecticut Residential Electrician".

Using your keywords periodically is essential for good on-page SEO (which I won't get into here. There are plenty of articles online showing you good SEO practices).

Once you've created your website, added pages and created a menu, you'll need to populate your site with some unique articles. Create 10 different articles that are anywhere between 500-1,500 words each. These articles can answer common questions, or cover news within that industry. The most important thing to keep in mind is that your content has to be relevant and written with a user in mind.

Examples of content that I created on another website I own – dentalwebsitedesign.com include articles about the .DENTIST domain names, how to improve a dental website within minutes and responsive website design. These are all relevant to the industry and answer questions that a user may have.

Once you've created your articles, post one per day for the next five days. Then, one per week for the next five weeks. Along with other SEO methods, this should help you to get ranked for your relevant keywords. Here's an SEO checklist that I follow:

http://www.clickminded.com/seo-checklist/

The point of writing these long articles is to give some weight to your site. If Google sees that you are actively contributing unique content to that niche, then you're more likely to appear for relevant searches.

There are, of course, other things you need to do to your website such as adding images (which can be downloaded for free from a site such as Pixabay.com) and writing page content – such as a services page. Check online for ideas of what to add to your site, or check out a competitor's website to see what they do. You might also get article ideas this way.

If you're using BlackRiders theme, you'll notice that in Appearance → Theme Options → General Settings there is a box which says Top Right Contact Details. A phone number should go here.

But how do you get a phone number in the first place, and where should it be directed? Your answer is Twilio.com. Twilio lets you rent a phone number for as little as $1 per month, and can let you choose from various area codes, and even toll-free numbers. So for my ConnecticutElectrician.com site, I'd chose an 860 area code number as this a

Connecticut area code. When you've found a partner to provide leads to, you can forward this number to their phone number and monitor the number of calls via Twilio.

The next thing you need to do is find a partner to sell these leads to. This should be a fairly easy thing to do. Take a look through Google for sites that are either advertising for your keywords, or who are on page 2 or lower.

The reason why I say page 2 or lower is that any listing on page 1 should be considered a direct competitor to you – you're trying to outrank those websites, so partnering with them wouldn't make sense. The chances are that those who are advertising for the keywords, or who are on page 2 or lower would jump at the chance of getting leads from you.

Choose one company – check their reviews, trustworthiness and examples of their work (if possible) to see whether they're a reputable company. If they are, find the email address of their CEO/Owner (if you read the domain sales guide, you'll know how to go about doing this) and email them asking them whether they'd like more business leads.

Explain to them that you have a website up and running which you'll be collecting leads from. In most cases, they'll reply saying that they're interested in working with you. From here you can work out details such as how leads will be delivered, whether you'll forward your Twilio number to their own number and what your commission or cost will be.

There are two ways of working out how you'll get paid. The first method is to get paid per lead sent, no matter whether they close a deal or not. You'll typically be paid a lower amount per lead versus the second option of a commission. The great thing about being paid per lead is that you don't need to worry about tracking the leads at all, and you're not concerned about whether a deal has been closed or not. You'll get paid no matter what.

Option two – commission – will give you a higher earning, but it will all depend on how good the company you're working with is at closing their sales. You won't be paid per lead, but you'll be paid a commission (usually around 20%) of their net profit on that deal when you provide a successful lead. Option two means you'll have to do more work to track the lead and guarantee that the sale has been successful, but it also means a potentially higher earning for you.

It's entirely up to you how you go about this. The company you're working with may have a preference as to which option you agree on, but in the end you're the one providing leads for them, this should be done under your terms.

If you find out that you aren't being paid for leads that you provide, then move on to another company. You're in control!

You'll need to work hard to make sure that you do continue to capture leads on any domain name that you develop in this way. I'd recommend adding new, relevant content to your sites at least once per week.

I've personally only created a couple of successful lead generation websites, and I'm by no means an expert on lead generation – I'm constantly learning about web design, development and SEO, but from my two projects I have been able to pick up the knowledge that I've shared with you here.

By creating a website which is generating leads, you're also increasing the value of your domain name. If you do decide to sell your website, you can go to an end user and tell them that it's #1 in search rankings for a specific term, and it's generating leads every month.

Affiliate Websites

The second domain development method is to create an affiliate website. An affiliate website allows you to create a site which promotes another company's product. If someone buys a product from your website using your unique affiliate link, you'll get a commission.

A popular affiliate scheme is Amazon.com's affiliate program. I recently read an article about a woman who created 40 websites promoting various Amazon products, and is making over $10,000 per month from this.

Aside from expert keyword research, her secret was content creation. She had websites with hundreds of pages of content at between 600 to 1000 words per article. Her articles concentrated on reviewing 3-5 products per article, using affiliate links to send visitors to Amazon.

If you have any exact match domains, or product domain names then you may wish to consider creating an affiliate site – especially if you can find an affiliate program with a good commission rate.

Directories

Directories used to be a very popular way to monetize your domain names a couple of years ago – especially geographical domain names. Create a local listings website on your domain name, add regular content and attract companies to add their websites to your directory.

I say that directories *used* to be a popular monetization method. I don't see directories as being a worthwhile way of trying to monetize a domain name anymore. I've found that a majority of users who may have visited directory sites in the past to find links to local businesses will now use Yelp, Google or Facebook. Local businesses know this and most have these bases covered.

You'll also have the problem of needing visitors in order to attract business listings, but you'll need business listings in order to attract visitors.

Hiring Freelancers

The Internet is full of freelancers that can do just about anything – write your content, design your websites, do SEO, design logos, and plenty more. The point is – should you hire freelancers to build and develop your sites for you?

It's something that you may consider in the future, but if you're just starting out, learn how to do it yourself. Aside from being a useful skill, you may find that you enjoy the challenge of writing website content, or creating a logo for your website.

The main things to learn yourself are:

1. How to install WordPress. I use WordPress for every development project, as it's so easy to use. If you've never used WordPress before, start out by installing a WordPress site on one of your domain names. Learn the administration system, familiarize yourself with plugins and themes, and set up a website for yourself.
2. How to create engaging content. Just start to write & research, and you'll find yourself finishing your first 1,000 word article in no time at all. Make this a daily or weekly practice and you'll soon be writing captivating articles.
3. Basic coding. It's useful to know the basics of HTML and CSS to be able to customize

WordPress themes and to make adjustments to plugins. There are some free courses on Udemy.com which can teach you the basics that you need.

4. SEO. The term SEO stands for search engine optimization. It's a topic which is constantly evolving thanks to Google's search engine adjustments. You don't need to know advanced SEO practices – just essentials such as putting your keywords into page headers, keyword density etc.

If you do manage to master these techniques, you'll find that you can create websites whenever you want on whatever subject you want. You won't have to wait for various companies to complete your work and you won't have to pay content writers.

Of course, you may get to the point where you've found a system that works for you and you want to create more websites. At this point it may make sense for you to outsource the work. If you get to this point, I'd recommend using a website such as oDesk.com to find reliable freelancers to work with.

Finding a reliable, talented freelancer can be difficult. Making sure that you look through reviews of their work and their portfolio can give you an idea of the level they're at. Asking them relevant questions about your project may also give you a sense of how knowledgeable they are on that subject.

Chapter 11: Further Reading

I hope that this book has been of some use to you, and you've got some excellent pointers as to how to start domaining successfully, or how to improve your existing domain portfolio. This shouldn't be the end of your domain related reading, and as you'll no doubt be aware by now, the domain industry is constantly changing, so it's important to keep up to date with the latest news if you want any chance of being successful.

There are a few resources that I mentioned earlier in the book that I recommend you look at daily or weekly. To save you going back to that chapter, I will post my recommendations here again.

NamePros.com: Around 1 million domain investors are registered on NamePros, making it the

largest free domain name forum online. It's an excellent place to buy, sell and discuss domain names with like-minded individuals.

DNForum: This is the leading domain name forum, and there are enough current discussions and domain sales to keep you visiting the website every couple of days. There isn't as much activity on there as there was a year or two ago, but with the popularity of Facebook, Twitter, LinkedIn and alike that isn't surprising.

There are also plenty of interesting discussions in the archives to look through, which you can access by searching on DNForum.com. If you have any questions about domaining, the chances are that someone has asked them and they've been answered on DNForum.com.

There is a one off payment to access the Gold, Platinum or Exclusive membership levels.

DomainSherpa.com: Run by Michael Cyger, this site contains some fantastic resources for domaining. There are hundreds of hours of interviews with successful domainers for you to listen to as well as weekly domain portfolio reviews and domain news discussions. I can almost guarantee you'll learn something new every time you log onto the site.

There's also a domain name tax guide available to buy on DomainSherpa.com, which is written by a certified accountant and edited by a former IRS agent. It's worth getting if you have any concerns about how to classify your domain names in tax returns.

Domaining.com: You may already be aware of domaining.com, but if you're not it's a news aggregator – essentially pooling in domain name related news from a number of blogs and news websites. I visit it a couple of times every day, as this is where you'll find the latest sales statistics, opinion articles, drop lists and more.

DNJournal: Ron Jackson's website has been a stalwart of the domain name industry for over ten years, posting weekly domain name sales charts and keeping track of vital statistics which help every domain name investor whether you know it or not. Ron produces a new domain sales chart every Thursday. This is where you can find out the type of domain names that are selling well at the moment.

www.ingramcontent.com/pod-product-compliance
Lightning Source LLC
Chambersburg PA
CBHW030613220526
45463CB00004B/1280